SOCIALISM: FROM THE ABOLITIONISTS TO OBAMA

Gary Lee Roper
7/1/2010

Copyright 2010
House of Nathan Publishing

All Rights Reserved

ISBN 978-0-9828422-0-1

Acknowledgement

Throughout this book you will find somewhat lengthy quotes from many who are authorities in their fields. There is, of course, a reason for this.

My field of proficiency is Theology, in addition to practical consumer economics dealing with taxes, credit, insurance, and investments. I am not an economic theorist nor philosopher. Neither am I a scientist nor climatologist. Therefore, I will quote from experts in various fields without apology. In doing this I follow the admonition of that great nineteenth century "prince of preachers," Charles Haddon Spurgeon who said:

> He who never quotes will never be quoted.
> He who never reads will never be read.
> He who refuses to use the brains of others proves that he has no brains of his own.

Gary Lee Roper, DD, DBA
Southaven, Mississippi
June 2010

Favorite quote to discredit socialism:

"It is untrue that some are poor because others are rich. If an order of society in which incomes were equal replaced the capitalist order, everyone would become poorer."

Ludwig von Mises

Table of Contents

Preface	4
Socialism or Communism?	6
Development of Liberalism	41
Socialism and Property	73
Socialism and Education	87
Socialism and the Church	118
Why Socialism Will Not Work	157
Global Warming and the Communist Agenda	164
Socialism and the War Against God	188
Appendix A: Carroll Quigley	195
Appendix B: The Invisible Government	210
Appendix C: The Pulpit as the Moral Conscience of the Nation by Dr. W. R. Downing	202
Bibliography	207
Index	211

PREFACE

> The American people will never knowingly adopt Socialism, but under the name of liberalism they will adopt every fragment of the socialist program until one day America will be a socialist nation without ever knowing how it happened. –Norman Thomas

The cover of the February16, 2009 issue of NEWSWEEK magazine pronounced: "We are all socialists now."

The prophecy of Norman Thomas came to fulfillment finally in the year 2009. *Our* form of Socialism did not come directly from Europe; its seeds were sown in New England during the first half of the nineteenth century. Now, under Barack Hussein Obama the Socialist dream that has been developing in our country for over one hundred seventy years has come to complete realization.

Our only hope of reversing the loss of liberty and freedom in this nation is to learn how it happened. We cannot place any hope whatsoever in either one of our political parties. Norman Thomas had both parties pegged right when he said, "The difference between Democrats and Republicans is that Democrats have accepted some ideas of socialism cheerfully, while Republicans have accepted them reluctantly."

The Democratic Party of today is as far removed from Thomas Jefferson as daylight is from darkness. In fact, the Democrat Party follows the vision of Jefferson's rival, Alexander Hamilton, and yet they fail to do justice to Hamilton.

The Republican Party, also known as the Red Republican Party, was formed in 1854 as the party of the radical abolitionists. Over a period of time, the parties switched position as the Democrats became more radical and the Republicans became mildly conservative or mainstream.

Today, neither party offers the true American constitutionalist any hope. The late Samuel T. Francis once bewailed that Americans don't have two ideologically dissimilar political parties. Rather we have an evil party (the "liberals") and a stupid party (the "conservatives").

SOCIALISM OR COMMUNISM?

The ancient Greek philosopher, Plato, advocated a form of a socialistic state as revealed in his book on political theory, *The Republic* written around 380 B. C. The idea that the child belongs to the state, which is a basic premise for our public government school system was borrowed from this work.

Aristotle was a profound critic of Plato's socialistic theory. He believed that those who contributed the most support and good for the country should be the beneficiaries of its wealth and influence.

The early church at Jerusalem established a socialistic society as recorded in the book of Acts, chapter four. However, this experiment took place without God's sanction or command and soon failed never to be repeated again.

What is the difference between socialism and communism? The ultimate goal of socialism and communism is essentially the same differing only in the method of achievement.

SOCIALISM has been defined as an economic and political hypothesis that supports governmental ownership and administration of the method in which goods are produced and distributed. Private ownership is unacceptable and not allowed. Robert Owen (1771 –1858), born in Wales, was a social reformer and one of the founders of socialism. He is sometimes referred to as "the father of socialism." His philosophy was based on three tenets: (1) Man is not accountable for his own will and deeds for the reason that his total make-up comes into being independently of himself; that is, he is a product of his environment. Consequently he supported education and labour reform as a way of improving society. (2) All religions are in the imagination of man. (3) Instead of the factory system of labor, which greatly exploited the worker in Owen's time, he supported the "putting-out" or sub-contracting system.

CHRISTIAN SOCIALISM or "Christian Socialist," is a term that is encountered from time to time and must be expounded upon. It was prevalent in 19th century Europe, but there are Christian Socialist political parties in Europe today. Actually the word is an oxymoron; a contradiction in terms, like a "wise fool" or a "legal murderer." Christian Socialism was denounced in 1878 by Pope Leo XIII in the papal encyclical *Quod Apostolici Muneris*.[1]

THE FABIAN SOCIETY originated in England. It is an outgrowth of the Fellowship of the New Life (founded 1883 under the influence of Thomas Davidson). The society was built up the following year by Frank Podmore and Edward Pease. George Bernard Shaw and Sidney Webb became members soon thereafter and were committed to its goals. Recognition was attained when the *Fabian Essays* (1889), were published with essays by Shaw, Webb, Annie Besant, and Graham Wallas. The Fabians disagreed with Karl Marx's ideas of the inevitability of violent class struggle, stressing that social reforms and infiltration of all present social and political institutions would bring about the natural development of socialism. They ignored trade unionism and other labor movements until Beatrice Potter (who later married Sidney Webb) joined the group. They subsequently helped create (1900) the unified Labour Representation Committee, which developed into the Labour party. The Labour party adopted their main views,

---

[1] "Socialism & the Vatican," *Time* magazine, July 8, 1957.

but the Fabian Society lingers as an associated research and publicity organization.[2]

COMMUNISM is a system of government in which the state plans and controls the economy, and a single, often authoritarian party, holds power, claiming to make progress toward a higher social order in which all goods are equally shared by the people. The writings of Karl Marx (1818-1883), a communist revolutionary, inspired the foundation of many communist regimes in the twentieth century. The basis of his thought was something he called "dialectical materialism." Actually it was a combination of the ideas of two other philosophers, Georg Wilhelm Friedrich Hegel (1770-1831), and Ludwig Andreas von Feuerbach (1804–1872).

In the most basic of terms, he and his cohort, Fredrick Engels (1820-1895) borrowed from Hegel dialectics, the technique of reasoning that aims to comprehend things concretely in all their movement, change and interconnection, with their opposite and contradictory sides in unity.[3] From philosopher and anthropologist Ludwig Feuerbach was borrowed materialism: nothing exists but matter, that which can be experienced with the senses. Taking dialectics, or duality, which is based on opposites, they advanced the idea that if a thesis is presented and another is given in opposition to it (the anti-thesis), the two would blend together to create a new assemblage called a synthesis.

Capitalism and Communism are opposites. Traditionally America has been the great bastion of Capitalism. We have seen corporations and banks fail requiring government bail-outs

---

[2] The Columbia Encyclopedia, Sixth Edition Copyright© 2004, Columbia University Press.
[3] MIA: Encyclopedia of Marxism: http://www.marxists.org/glossary/terms/d/i.htm

naturally will translate into more government control. Government intrudes more with each passing year into our lives with all kinds of regulation and taxation. We elected a president like Barack Obama. Are we seeing the melding of the thesis and the anti-thesis to form the synthesis?

Going back in history, Communism has differed from socialism in method as both violence and genocide are acceptable means to an end. The difference between socialism and communism may be likened unto the difference between the Unitarians and the Transcendentalists of the nineteenth century. The Transcendentalists were willing to go further in the pursuit of Utopia than were the Unitarians. The Transcendentalist, Theodore Parker, in a letter to Francis Jackson written from Rome in 1859 advocated the murder of the slaveholders (*Antebellum Slavery*, 117). In like manner the communists will proceed with their goal utilizing drastic and brutal methods.

William Tecumseh Sherman shared some of the communistic philosophy. It is no wonder then, as to why he was so eager to make war on Southern civilians; to murder, steal, burn, and destroy. Sherman wrote his wife that the purpose of the war was "extermination, not of soldiers alone, that is the least of the trouble, but the people. . ." of the South (*Citizen Sherman*, 152).

> There is a class of people [in the South] men, women, and children, who must be killed or banished before you can hope for peace and order. (152)

Sherman's burning of libraries and court houses that contained valuable history and records was truly Marxist philosophy. Karl Marx, as a correspondent for the New York *Tribune* newspaper of

Horace Greeley, from 1852-1861 noted that people who are separated from their history are easily persuaded.

Sherman hated the white Southerner who opposed strong central government. He despised the Negro and loathed the Jew. Sherman steadfastly refused to lead Negro troops in his army. He said, "Soldiers must do many things without orders from their own sense. Negroes are not equal to this (5)."

Sherman informed Hallack that he intended to march, in the future as in the past, at the head of a lily white army. When some of Sherman's letters were leaked to the press in the North, he said, "I never thought my nigger letter would get into the press (160-161)." After Mr. Lincoln's War, his next task was the genocide of the American Indian, which he referred to as the "final solution." He wrote in a letter to Grant, "We must act with vindictive earnestness against the Sioux, even to their extermination, men, women, and children. (264)."

Failed nineteenth century American experiments in Socialism are revealed in Thomas Bailey's history, *The American Pageant, 3rd edition*.

> Professional "do-gooders" popped up at every hand, giving to the 1840s the distinction of being the "hot air period" of American history. About everything was tried, from communism to socialism. . . . Various reformers, ranging from the high-minded to the "lunatic fringe" set up more than forty communities of a . . . communistic . . . nature. Robert Owen established, in 1825, a communal society of about a thousand persons at New Harmony Indiana. The enterprise sank in a morass of contradiction and confusion.

> Brook Farm in Massachusetts, comprising two hundred acres was started in 1841 with the cooperation of about twenty intellectuals. They prospered reasonably well until 1846. . . . The whole experiment in "plain living and high thinking," then collapsed in debt.
>
> A more radical experiment was the Oneida Colony, founded in New York in 1848. It practiced free love, birth control, and the eugenic selection of parents to produce superior offspring. The leader finally fled to Canada to escape prosecution for adultery. In 1879-1880, the group embraced monogyny and abandoned communism. (368)

The Brook Farm experiment was supported by three famous Transcendentalists: Ralph Waldo Emerson, Henry David Thoreau, and Nathaniel Hawthorne. Most all of Hawthorne's friends including Emerson were rabid abolitionists. Hawthorne himself was not an abolitionist and was not keen about the war against the Southern states. He was also very critical of Abraham Lincoln but most of his written articles belittling Lincoln were edited and repressed.

Not only were most of the rabid abolitionists Unitarians and Transcendentalists, they were communistic and socialistic in their mindset. Their goals for establishing a Utopia were the same goals as today's socialists, including Barack Hussein Obama.

It must be stated that *not every* abolitionist was a communist or a socialist. However, the utopian goal that characterized the abolitionist movement *as a whole* was socialistic. They wanted strong centralized government, government controlled education or rather indoctrination, confiscation and redistribution of wealth, and an end to *orthodox* Christianity.

☞ "The American socialist party is merely carrying on the work of Abolitionist, John Brown." Eugene Debs, 19th century American socialist.

When one does research, one may find names that do not belong on lists of abolitionists such as Benjamin Franklin, Alexander Hamilton, and Ulysses Grant. Grant even said of his service (1861-1865) *"If I thought this war would free the negro I would put my sword in its scabbard and go home."*[4]

Among well known abolitionists were: John Brown, Theodore Parker, George L. Stearnes, Franklin B. Sanborn, Dr. Samuel Gridley Howe, Gerrit Smith, Rev. Thomas Wentworth Higginson, Henry Wordsworth Longfellow, Julia Ward Howe, Horace Greeley, Louisa May Alcott, Susan B. Anthony, Angelina Grimke, Henry Ward Beecher, Benjamin Butler, Lyman Beecher, Cassius Clay, William Ellery Channing, Ralph Waldo Emerson, Charles Finney, Wendell Phillips, Thaddeus Stevens, Harriet Beecher Stowe, Henry David Thoreau, John Greenleaf Whittier, William Lloyd Garrison, and Samuel Joseph May.

Samuel Joseph May (1797-1871) was a Unitarian minister who called for a socialistic government and the redistribution of wealth. He aided Horace Mann in the government control of education His records may be found in the Boston Public Library and the Massachusetts Historical Society.

---

[4] J. Clarence Stonebraker, *The Unwritten South: Cause, Progress and Result of the Civil War--Relics of Hidden Truth After Forty Years*, Hagerstown, Maryland: Hagerstown Bookbinding and Printing, 1903.

James H. Thornwell, (1812-1862) a South Carolina Presbyterian scholar and educator, in speaking of the abolitionist movement said in 1850:

> The parties in this conflict are not merely abolitionists and slaveholders—they are atheists, socialists, communists, Red Republicans, Jacobins on the one side, and friends of order and regulated freedom on the other.

The charge of socialism of the abolitionists came from the North also as revealed in the Northern newspapers:

The New York Herald   Friday, October 25, 1850

Women's Rights Convention

Awful Combination of Socialism, Abolitionism, and Infidelity

Bible and Constitution Repudiated

Worcester, Mass. Oct. 23, 1850.

That motley mingling of abolitionists, socialists, and infidels, of all sexes and colors, called the Women's Rights Convention, assembled in this city, to-day, and an account of their proceedings we have the honor herewith to communicate to the New York Herald.

Abby Kelly Foster--I do not talk of woman's rights, but of human rights, the rights of human beings. I do not come to ask [for] them, but to demand them; not to get down on my knees and beg for them, but to claim them. "Sauce for the goose is sauce for the gander." We have our rights, and the right to revolt, as did our fathers against King George the Third--the right to rise up and cut the tyrants' throats. On this subject I scorn to talk like a woman. We must give them the truth, and not twaddle. We must not be mealy mouthed with our tyrants in broadcloth and tight clothes. In short, in the harangue of Abby, she simply demanded that men and women should be treated as human beings all alike--that the sexes should be forgotten in society--that property and votes and offices, civil, religious and military, even to the right of cutting throats, should belong to woman as well as to man. She urged that the work should be commenced by educating both sexes together, and that all distinction in society between man and woman should be abolished, and that a woman was just as well qualified to be President as a man. [Applause.]

Charles C. Burleigh (an improved specimen of George H. Munday, the prophet having more beard and a greater amount of hair about his ears) next took the rostrum. He did not exactly agree with Mrs. Abby Kelly Foster, that the sexes should be dispensed with in the reorganization of society. He thought the two sexes were different, and that man and woman were sexes in soul as well as in body. He, however, agreed that the restraints upon woman ought to be removed, and that her freedom to choose her own vocation in life ought to be allowed upon an enlarged scale, as well as the privilege of the ballot box, the right of property, and so forth.

Recess till seven o'clock.

EVENING MEETING.
Hall crowded to excess.

Lucretia Mott was determined not to ask as a boon what she could demand as a right. She complained that woman's labor was not appreciated--that she was a slave, and the slave of superstition, and paid too much devotion to the Bible. Let theology take care of itself. Theology had always given way when compelled to do it by the light of truth, as in the case of George Combe and phrenology. He was first attacked, and then the theologians found out, when science was too strong for them, that it [phrenology] was according to revelation. (Laughter) She thought the right of woman to cut throats, in resisting despotism, was a debatable question because many contend for the doctrine of moral suasion. But in demanding woman's rights, she wanted no twaddle, no milk-and-water, but the plain and naked truth.

Mr. Wendell Phillips offered a series of resolutions: [here follows the text of the resolutions as subsequently published in the proceedings.] Mr. Phillips argued these several points at length, maintaining that the cobwebs and the superstitions of the Bible ought to be swept away. Woman, without culture, without capital, and shut off from commerce, the mechanic arts, the professions, and politics, dwindles down, like the poor colored man in slavery, into an inferior caste. He wished her to be mingled up in society, in the trial by jury, in representation, and in suffrage for her self defense. We should not give too much reverence to the law; laws were but pieces of paper, signed by Millard Fillmore (applause) and public opinion is the silliest thing in the world. (Laughter) He spoke with energy, urging that to secure woman's rights, it was necessary to break down the barriers of the law and the Bible, of feudal and Hebrew despotism, and begin at the very foundation of society.

Mrs. Rose--We are not contending here for the rights of the women of New England, or of old England, but of the world. And our greatest opposition is from the prejudice of our own sex. Man is as much the victim of his despotism as woman. We had heard a great deal of our Pilgrim Fathers; but who ever tells us anything of our pilgrim mothers? And were not their trials, and is not their glory equally great. Two positions we have assigned to woman.

Either to play the puppet in the parlor, or the drudge in the kitchen. And till all these old prejudices, and restrictions, and this whole system of woman's slavery from beginning to end, were done away with, and not till then, would man and woman be brought to a happy state of existence. (Applause.)

Mrs. Lucretia Mott--It strikes me, Madame President, that Mrs. Rose has made a better apology for man than he could make for himself. (Laughter) Woman is crushed, but nobody is to blame; it is circumstances that have crushed her. So of the poor slave. He is crushed, but nobody crushed him. It just happened so. (Laughter) It is an abstract evil, that's all. When we begin to denounce the slaveholder as a man-stealer, all scripture had to be searched before people would believe it, or venture to use the term. And with us, it is monopolizing, despotic man that we have to deal with, in our exclusion from offices, from the schools and colleges. The learned philosopher then proceeded to show that the men would prefer to be called knaves, rather than such fools as the idea that his ignorance of her rights was the cause of woman's wrongs. Men are cunning and crafty. They are not such innocent Abigails as you would suppose. (Laughter) She recommended agitation of woman's rights. It was the agitation of the slavery question that had shaken the capitol to its foundations, and that was the cause of the good fruit it will bring forth, in the liberation of the Southern slave. (Applause)

Wendell Phillips contended that woman was largely responsible for her grievances. In the marriage ceremony it is woman that declares she will love, honor, and obey. It was the assent and the prejudice of woman that were the greatest obstacles to her rights.

Mrs. Abby Kelly Foster took up the glove. Woman is a slave, and is obedient in the presence of her master. Ask the slave of Henry Clay, in his master's presence, if he is satisfied and happy; he will say yes. So with woman, though she might not get a cowhiding like the slave if she answered no! Still, she would be fearful to displease her husband, her lord and master, as he is. And her whole life, and her whole education was adapted to please him and serve him like a slave. And do you suppose that woman so situated can dare to assert her rights. If disobedient, she is fearful she will never get a husband. But don't believe her when she ridicules this movement or opposes it. She is a slave, and has to do it. Our only safety is to rebuke the oppressor, and to demand our rights.

Lucretia Mott--My friend, Wendell Phillips, says that it is the woman in marriage who says that she will "love, honor, and obey." As I understand it, the priest says the words, and she only answers "yes." (Laughter) The priest says "love, honor, and obey." Woman has been taught to pin her faith to the sleeve of the priest. Now, in our society [i.e., the Society of Friends to she belonged], there is nothing of this; but perfect equality and reciprocity. It is all the result of education. Sometime ago, if a woman could make a shirt, turn a pancake, and write her name at her marriage, she was educated. But she is beginning to understand that she is entitled to something more.

Mr. Foster (husband of Abby Kelly, a tall, ungainly figure, in big whiskers and spectacles) next took the platform. He was proceeding to remark that the question of woman's right to take the sword was irrelevant to the objects of the meeting, when

Mr. Burleigh raised a question of order against the Speaker himself. His object, however, was to move when the meeting adjourned that it adjourn to meet again at half-past nine in the morning. Agreed to.

Wm. Lloyd Garrison gave notice that the friends of the abolition of the gallows would meet at half-past eight.

Mr. Foster (husband of Abby Kelly), returned to the question of woman's right to use the sword. He thought it ought to be left an open question, for there were a million and a half of women in the South, in a condition makes us shudder to think of, and God only knows how soon the sword may be drawn for their deliverance, and I would not like to see her hands tied in the struggle. For this reason he considered it inexpedient to discuss the question of woman's right to use the sword. After a long rigmarole on woman hugging her chains, he concluded by charging that the pulpit and St. Paul were responsible for the enslavement of the sex. When the priest says to the woman, "Love, honor, and obey," what can she do?

Abby Kelly Foster--Do! Do as the wife of the Rev. Joseph Bancroft, of Worcester, did. Say "I won't." (Laughter) She was a good woman, and a much better man than her son George. She said I won't," and she compelled them to leave that part out.

Mr. Foster (husband to Abby Kelly)--yes; and there was a lady of seventy years old at dinner to-day, who said when she came to the word "obey," she dropped her husband's hand. (Laughter) The orator then went on to show that many women who did not appear so, were friends of this movement. He was once lecturing on the necessity of dissolving the Union, to get rid of the curse of slavery, when a man who dared not openly avow it, slipped a three dollar bill into his hand very quietly. So there are women who dare not speak, who will slip a three dollar bill to the advocate of woman's rights, if they had a chance.

Very stout lady, in a grey dress--My friend says that many a woman will slip a three dollar bill to the advocate of her rights. She cannot do it for she cannot get the three dollars, if she has a husband. (Laughter)

Mr. Foster--Ah, yes, I should have said if she can get it. He next argued that the slavery of woman degraded both sexes, and man the most, for that woman was naturally better than man.

And at a quarter past ten P.M. the Convention adjourned, to meet again at half past nine in the morning, to finish up the resolutions

It is quite apparent from the reading of the previous primary resource material that the Reverend James H. Thornwell hit the nail on the head when he called these people atheists and socialists. The radicals in this convention covered by the *New York Herald* attacked the Bible, St Paul, Judaism, Roman Catholicism, and all Christians.

Soon after emancipation, the abolitionists forsook the Negro and concentrated on Feminism and Temperance. Perhaps this is why Richard Harvey Cain, a Negro editor in Charleston, South Carolina observed in 1871:

> When the smoke and fighting is over, the Negroes have gained nothing and the whites have nothing left, while the jackals have all the booty. (*Antebellum Slavery*, 145, 146)

With regard to *FEMINISM*, the capability of women in teaching, nursing, and many other area of service outside the home is completely granted. However, women are out of place working in a coal mine or serving in combat situations in the military. Nonetheless, the highest calling of a married woman is in raising children and in keeping the home. This is the greatest sphere of influence.

THE TEMPERANCE MOVEMENT violated many liberties, was not really for temperance, but for total abstinence. Although the Bible condemns drunkenness, it does not teach total abstinence. Certainly it is true that one who never takes the first drink will never be a drunkard, but it is the sin of the heart that damns and results in immorality. If we desire the salvation of the soul, we need to get to the root of the problem. The temperance movement's solution was merely cutting sprouts. One can go to hell sober as well as drunk.

THE FORTY-EIGHTERS were European immigrants, most of whom, *but not all*, were Germans. These ideologues supported the revolutions that swept Europe in 1848. After the failure of their cause in Europe, many of these revolutionaries fled to America in hopes of promoting their socialistic and communistic ideas.

Charles A. Dana, a member of the Fourier Communistic Society and a close friend of Karl Marx, became Assistant Secretary of War under Abraham Lincoln after working with Horace Greeley, a dedicated socialist, with the *New York Tribune*. The man in charge of Lincoln's personal safety, Allan Pinkerton, had socialistic leanings and was an admirer of the essays of George Julian Harney, a friend of Marx and Engels.[5] More in depth information concerning the "forty-eighters" is covered in the book by Walter Kennedy and Al Benson, Jr., *Red Republicans and Lincoln's Marxists*. From this book, we read, "Marx understood that the proletarian revolution in America could not take place until after the emancipation of the slaves. [Marx states,] "Labor cannot emancipate itself in the white skin where in the black it is branded (32)."

Forty-eighters along with the abolitionists wanted to end slavery not out of compassion for the Negro, but to further the cause of socialism or communism. Communist Carl Schurz (a forty-eighter) was very influential in persuading Lincoln to issue the Emancipation Proclamation.

---

[5] Walter D. Kennedy and Al Benson, Red Republicans and Lincoln's Marxists, 107.

Among the Marxists officers in Lincoln's army were: Brigadier General Joseph Weydemeyer, a close friend of Karl Marx and Frederick Engels, Brigadier General Louis Blenker, Major General August Willich, Major Robert Rosa, Colonel Richard Hinton, Brigadier General Carl Schurz, Major General Franz Siegel, Commander Friedrich Karl Franz Hecker, Captain Gustav von Struve, Chief of Staff Alexander Asboth, Brevet Major Frederick Charles Salomon, and Colonel Fritz Annecke.

Was Abraham Lincoln a Marxist? Lincoln was a shrewd and devious politician. I would not say that he was actually a communist or a socialist; he was a centrist progressive. However, he certainly associated with them, did have dealings with them, and furthered their cause when it furthered his cause.

The republic of our founding fathers was destroyed and the constitution trampled upon by Abraham Lincoln. He confiscated firearms in violation of the Second Amendment. He took away personal liberties while increasing the power of centralized government and created the first progressive income tax. Opposition was squashed by suspending the Writ of Habeas Corpus. Newspaper editors that dared to criticize his policies were imprisoned and over one hundred newspapers were shut down. Obviously, Lincoln was a warmonger who believed in total war. His friendship with Karl Marx is demonstrated by the following correspondence:

> Sir:
> We congratulate the American People upon your re-election by a large Majority.
>
> If resistance to the Slave Power was the reserved Watchword of your first election, the triumphant war-cry of your re-election is, Death to Slavery.

From the commencement of the Titanic American Strife, the Working men of Europe felt instinctively that the Star Spangled Banner carried the Destiny of their class. The Contest for the territories opened the dire epopee, Was it not to decide whether the virgin soil of immense tracts should be wedded to the Labour of the Emigrant, or prostituted by the Tramp of the Slave Driver?

When an Oligarchy of 300,000 Slave-holders dared to inscribe, for the first time in the annals of the World, Slavery on the Banner of Armed Revolt; when on the very spots where hardly a century ago the idea of one great democratic Republic had first sprung up. Whence the first Declaration of The Rights of Man was issued, and the first impulse given to the European Revolution of the 18th Century; When on those very spots counter revolution, with systematic thoroughness, gloried in rescinding "The ideas entertained at the time of the formation of the old Constitution" and maintained "Slavery to be a beneficent Institution, indeed the only solution of the great problem of the relation of Labour to Capital," and cynically proclaimed property in Man "The corner stone of the New Edifice"; Then the Working Classes of Europe understood at once, Even before the fanatic partisanship of the Upper Classes for the confederate gentry had given its dismal warning, That the Slaveholder's Rebellion was to sound the tocsin for a general holy Crusade of Property against Labour, and that for the Men of Labour, with their hopes for the future, even their past conquests were at stake in that tremendous Conflict on the other side of the Atlantic. Everywhere they bore therefore patiently the hardships imposed upon them by the Cotton crisis, opposed enthusiastically the Pro Slavery Intervention, importunities of their "betters," and from most parts of Europe contributed their quota of blood to the good cause.

While the Working Men, the true political power of the North, allowed Slavery to defile their own Republic, while before the Negro, mastered and sold without his concurrence, they boasted it the highest prerogative of the white skinned Laborer to sell himself and choose his own Master, they were unable to attain the true Freedom of Labour or to support their European Brethren in their struggle for Emancipation, but this barrier to progress has been swept off by the red sea of Civil War.

The Working Men of Europe feel sure that as the American War of Independence initiated a new era of ascendancy for the Middle Class, so the American Anti-Slavery War will do for the Working Classes. They consider it an earnest of the epoch to come, that it fell to the lot of Abraham Lincoln, the single-minded Son of the Working Class, to lead his Country through the matchless struggle for the rescue of an enchained Race and the Reconstruction of a Social World.

—Karl Marx, "To Abraham Lincoln, President of the United States of America" (November 1864)

A direct line from the abolitionists to today's liberals is *The Nation*, a magazine founded by people who had been abolitionists and which is still in publication. The well-known socialist, Norman Thomas, served for a time as associate editor. The publication was founded in July of 1865 at 130 Nassau Street in Manhattan. Its founding coincided with the beginning of reconstruction in the Southern states, or as historian Thomas Bailey termed it, "re-destruction."

Notable contributors to *The Nation*: Leon Trotsky, Franklin D. Roosevelt, Jean-Paul Sartre, Bertrand Russell, Langston Hughes, James Baldwin, and Martin Luther King, Jr. The Federal Bureau of Investigation at one time looked closely at *The Nation* for "subversive" activism and ties.

Edward Bellamy published a utopian-socialist novel, *Looking Backward*, contrasted a peaceful, productive and happy socialist society in Boston at the end of the twentieth century with conditions of life at the end of the nineteenth century. Bellamy's work became the center of a movement called "nationalism." Nationalists clubs formed for discussing socialists ideas developed in middle-class circles in the early 1890s.

Edward Bellamy's cousin, Francis, a minister and prominent socialist, wrote a school pledge, the "Pledge of Allegiance" in 1892. This pledge now acknowledged as a part of American patriotism, was born out of concepts of political liberalism and socialism. Upon graduation as a ministerial student from the University of Rochester, he spoke at his commencement on the "Poetry of Human Brotherhood." In his speech, he applauded the concepts of the French Revolution. Later as a Baptist pastor in Little Falls, New York, he gave a speech to factory workers entitled, "Jesus the Socialist." In 1891, Bellamy was forced to resign as a Baptist pastor because of his socialist sermons and activities. He was denounced in 1928 by the Boston Baptist Union and the Daughters of the American Revolution for promoting anti-Christian, socialistic and communistic ideas.

Francis Bellamy was the author of the Pledge of Allegiance. The idea behind the pledge was to "promote the state's schools." The "pledge" as originally written:

> I pledge allegiance to my flag and to the republic for which it stands: one nation, indivisible, with liberty and justice for all."

The original salute was with the right hand outstretched and raised. The word *allegiance* was taken from Lincoln's "oath of allegiance" for rebellious Southerners. The word *indivisible* was in opposition to the concept of secession.

Francis Bellamy, along with his cousin, Edward Bellamy, became heroes of John Dewey and other advocates of "progressive education." In 1924 the DAR changed the wording from *my flag* to *the flag of the United States of America*. In 1954 the Congress, by the influence of the Roman Catholic Knights of Columbus added the words, "under God."

Henry George was born in Philadelphia, Pennsylvania to a lower middle-class family. He became an American writer, politician, and political economist with strong socialistic views. Dr. Francis Nigel Lee remarked in his book, *A Christian Introduction to the History of Philosophy:*

> Much subtler but perhaps even more dangerous were the views of the American social philosopher Henry George (1839-1899), who advocated the

nationalization of all land and its redistribution as the common property of all people and the establishment of the single tax. His views had much influence on British Socialists like William Morris and Fabians like George Bernard Shaw. (170)

The views of Henry George were expressed in his most famous work, *Progress and Poverty* written during 1879.

As the result of Mr. Lincoln's War, not only was the old South destroyed but the North has lost constitutional government and the door was opened for a socialist America. "Marx's idea of public education financed by the government also became a central part of part of Lincoln's agenda (Kennedy and Benson, 76)."

Edwin Stanton, Abraham Lincoln's Secretary of War had said, "Wars are not fought to defeat an enemy, wars are fought to create a condition."[6]

As stated, in 1862, in order to finance the war, the nation's first income tax law was made during Lincoln's administration. It was a prototype of our current income tax insomuch that it was founded on the laws of graduated, or progressive, taxation and of withholding income at the foundation. In 1862, a person earning from $600 to $10,000 per year was to pay tax at the rate of 3%. Those with incomes of more than $10,000 were to pay taxes at a higher rate. Additional sales and excise taxes were added, and an "inheritance" tax also made its first appearance. The Act of 1862 launched the office of Commissioner of Internal Revenue. The

---

[6] Des Griffin, *Midnight Messenger of Cultural Marxism*, Emissary Publications, P. O. Box 294, Colton, Oregon 97017

Commissioner was granted the authority to assess, levy, and collect taxes, and the right to enforce the tax laws through seizure of property and income and through prosecution. The powers and authority continue much the same today.

In 1868, Congress spotlighted its taxation efforts on tobacco and distilled spirits and eliminated the income tax in 1872. It had a short-lived revival in 1894 and 1895. In 1895, the U.S. Supreme Court decided that the income tax was unconstitutional because it was not shared out among the states in conformity with the Constitution.[7]

George Washington, and Andrew Jackson were strongly against a Central National Bank. In a letter to John Taylor in 1816, Jefferson conveyed this wariness, ". . . I sincerely believe, with you, that banking establishments are more dangerous than standing armies; and that the principle of spending money to be paid by posterity, under the name of funding, is but swindling futurity on a large scale." Additions were made to this quote, which made the rounds on the Internet; those additions were proven false by SNOPES. Do not be confused by this. The portion quoted above can be verified and I invite you to do so.

Today the Federal Reserve has the power to print an unlimited amount of "fiat currency" is nothing less than legalized counterfeiting. It is impossible to run a "welfare state" with hard currency.

---

[7]<http://www.infoplease.com/ipa/A0005921.html>

THE WILSON PRESIDENCY ADVANCES SOCIALISM

The Reverend Dr. Joseph Ruggles Wilson (1822-1903) was an Orthodox Presbyterian preacher of noble character and a very able and respected minister. However, it is sad that his son, Woodrow Wilson lacked many of his best attributes. The presidency of Woodrow Wilson advanced socialism in several ways. He pushed for creation of a central bank. On his march to advance socialism, Wilson initiated a heavy progressive or graduated income tax. To make sure that the Supreme Court could not again outlaw the tax, he was smart enough to get the 16th amendment to the Constitution approved in February of 1913.

Leon Trotsky been expelled from France in 1916 for his subversive activities. He had found political asylum in the United States of America under the Woodrow Wilson administration. In April of 1917, Wilson facilitated the entry of this radical revolutionary into Russia with an American passport. Trotsky then became one of the leaders in a bloody insurgency resulting in a Communist regime that terrorized the world for most of the twentieth century.

Perhaps the catalyst in the strange Wilson-Trotsky connection was a man who savored the role of "power behind the throne," Colonel Edward M. House (1857-1938). He really wasn't a colonel. It was an honorary title bestowed on him by a governor of Texas in gratitude for his help political contributions and aid. Colonel House was President Wilson's advisor and right hand man. Many years have passed since his days of mysterious sway over Woodrow Wilson and we can look back upon his legacy. It shall be left to the reader to draw conclusions about Colonel House, Woodrow Wilson, and the existence of a design by some concealed silhouette group to direct the affairs of this nation and the world.

Edward M. House was the son of a wealthy banker and land-owner who grew up in a Fabian household. He was educated in England because, as his father put it, he wanted to raise his sons to "know and serve England."[8] Under a pseudonym in 1912, House wrote *Philip Dru: Administrator*, a fictional account about a socialistic utopian society would evolve in the United States as a result of a infiltration of Democrat and Republican parties, rendering them essentially identical. Next would come a graduated federal income tax, a central bank, inheritance taxes, and taking away powers reserved for the states.[9] Allegedly, Franklin Delano Roosevelt was quite taken with this book.

Woodrow Wilson read *Philip Dru* after his November 1912 election while he was taking some time off.[10] Within a year, the Wilson administration had plans in place to entirely restructure the federal financial set-up in accordance with the notions outlined in the novel. Colonel House influenced President Wilson to agree to the ideas of Nelson Aldrich (a Rockefeller middle-man) to create a graduated **income tax** and the **Federal Reserve**.[11] From 1912-1914, Wilson's legislative program was principally the agenda from House's book.[12] During the winter of 1917-1918, he presided over a group of intellectuals and wealthy financiers who gathered in New York City to discuss plans to "make the world safe for democracy." Out of these think-tank "inquiries," as they were termed by the group, grew the **Council on Foreign Relations**, the

---

[8] Rose L. Martin, *Fabian Freeway: High Road to Socialism in the U.S.A.*, 160.
[9] Alan Stang, *The Actor: The True Story of John Foster Dulles, Secretary of State, 1953-1959,* Boston & Los Angeles: Western Islands, (1968).
[10] Robert F. Rifkind, "The Colonel's Dream of Power," *American Heritage,* 64 February 1959.
[11] (http://hubpages.com/hub/Nelson_Aldrich)
[12] Sigmund Freud and William C. Bullitt, *Thomas Woodrow Wilson: A Psychological Study* London: Weidenfeld & Nicolson, 152.

now powerful **CFR**.[13] House also was a member of the U.S. delegation to the Paris Peace Conference of 1919, and he worked closely with Wilson in drafting the covenant of the **League of Nations**.[14]

After Wilson was out of office the move toward a socialistic America slowed down somewhat.

Herbert Hoover and Franklin D. Roosevelt

Some sources claim that the same powerful forces that controlled Woodrow Wilson then raised Franklin D. Roosevelt to the presidency. Most people are aware of the socialism of FDR, but many are completely unaware of the destructive policies of this President. The policies of Hoover are described in the book written in 2009 by Thomas E. Woods, Jr., *Meltdown*:

> For decades, American schoolchildren were— many still are— taught that President Herbert Hoover, who is described as a strict proponent of laissez faire, sat back and did nothing as the Great Depression devastated the country. Only when Franklin Roosevelt took office in March 1933 was serious action taken to arrest the economy's decline. Although most schoolteachers perpetuate this myth even now, it would be considered embarrassing in historical circles to repeat his version of events today. Hoover expressly said that the laissez-faire approach to the economy was a thing of the past. No peacetime president in American history intervened in

---

[13] Peter Grose, *Continuing the Inquiry,* New York: Council on Foreign Relations, 1996, 2006.
[14] (http://www.answers.com/topic/house-edward-mandell) Britannica Concise Encyclopedia:

the economy to the extent that Hoover did. Among other things, he launched public works projects, raised taxes, extended emergency loans to failing firms, hobbled international trade, and lent money to the states for relief programs. He sought to prop up wages at a time when consumer prices were falling dramatically, thereby calling on firms in effect to give raises to their workers at a time of great business vulnerabilities. This is why Franklin Roosevelt accused Hoover, during the 1932 presidential campaign, of having presided over "the greatest spending administration in peacetime in all of history," and derided him for "believing that we ought to center control of everything in Washington as rapidly as possible." FDR's running mate, John Nance Garner, declared that Hoover was "leading the country down the path to socialism. Meanwhile the Depression just grew worse and worse.[15]

Upon election to the office of president, Roosevelt immediately implemented socialistic programs that were planned to hasten America down the Socialistic path. When the Union of Soviet Socialists Republics (USSR) were on a verge of total collapse, Roosevelt stepped in to save the march toward a global society of socialized authoritarianism. He granted the criminal state of the USSR official diplomatic recognition. This opened the credit markets of the world to Stalin and communist Russia. During the period from 1942 to 1945 the Roosevelt administration, via the Lend Lease program, covertly pumped twelve billion dollars (*1940s dollars*) into the Soviet Union. The Roosevelt administration control over propaganda can be viewed by watching old films.

---

[15] Thomas E. Woods, Jr., *Meltdown,* Washington, D. C. : Regnery Publishing, 2009, 99.

In 1943 Warner Brothers premiered *Mission to Moscow*, based on the book of the same name by Joseph E. Davies, U.S. ambassador to the Soviet Union from 1936 to 1938. The authors of *Hollywood Goes to War* characterize this picture as the "most notorious example of propaganda in the guise of entertainment ever produced by Hollywood." *Mission to Moscow* traces in pseudo-documentary style Davies' career as ambassador and the events taking place in the Soviet Union and worldwide from the mid-1930's through 1941.

The Roosevelt administration was intimately involved in the making of this picture, represented FDR as a great internationalist and anti-fascist. Davies had power of script approval and was ultimately responsible for *Mission to Moscow's* glossing over of Stalinist crimes. Davies insisted that the Soviet invasion of Finland be portrayed as happening at the "invitation" of Finland to the Soviets to occupy strategic positions against Germany. Likewise, other Soviet crimes of the 1930's are ignored or passed over: the invasion of the eastern portion of Poland in 1939, the aggression against Estonia, Latvia and Lithuania, and the forced collectivization of the kulaks (small farmers) in the Ukraine with the resulting starvation of millions of peasants. The film represented the Moscow purge trials as the result of attempts by Krestinsky and other "Old Bolsheviks" to sell out the Soviet Union to Germany and Japan. *Mission to Moscow* used documentary film footage to add verisimilitude to this vintage "docudrama," depicted the American isolationists as a small cabal plotting to thwart the people's will to "collective security." The Soviet Union was depicted as a land of plenty in contrast to National Socialist Germany's alleged chronic lack of food and consumer goods. The public was led to believe the Soviet Union was a "democracy" and the Russian people were "just like Americans."

> Most of the major studios produced pro-Soviet films in the last years of the war, including *Song of Russia* (MGM, 1943), *Three Russian Girls* (United Artists, 1943), *North Star* (MGM, 1943), *Boy from Stalingrad* (Columbia, 1943), *Days of Glory* (RKO, 1944) and *Counterattack* (Columbia, 1945). Hollywood had always claimed that it only gave the public what it wanted, and cited the movies' popularity as proof. But since the cartel controlled the range of choice, Hollywood was saying only that the public bought what it was given.[16]

On the home front, Roosevelt's programs made the Great Depression of the 1930s much worse. A short synopsis of the New Deal was summed up by Harry Hopkins, advisor to the president, in these words, "We shall tax and tax, and spend and spend, and elect and elect." (Thomas J. DiLorenzo, *How Capitalism Saved America,* 179).

"The Roosevelt administration spent record amounts and amassed record deficits between 1933 and the U. S. entry into World War II in 1941, but it failed to end the Great Depression in America. The unemployment rate was still in double digits (14.6% in 1940) on the eve of the war (DiLorenzo, *Hamilton's Curse,* 56)."

The failed theories of British economist John Maynard Keynes (1883-1946) taught that massive government spending could stimulate the economy and end the depression. The social programs of Roosevelt increased the national debt and brought no relief.

> President Franklin Roosevelt's New Deal was devastating and not just in the direct effect it had on the American economy of the 1930s. One of the most damaging side effects has been that it created the

---

[16] <http://www.ihr.org/jhr/v08/v08p104_Wikoff.html>

> expectation that government will step in to "solve" any economic crisis– it has fostered the myth that government intervention is necessary to counter the exploitative nature of capitalists. Thus government regulations now handcuff almost all industries, and virtually every day we hear calls for further regulation.
> (*How Capitalism Saved America*, 206)

Roosevelt's established the Agricultural Adjustment Act (AAA) that adopted a program to pay farmers to burn their crops and slaughter their livestock while many people were going hungry. Eventually he came up with a more practical plan and began paying farmers not to plant crops. This became known as "renting one's land out to the government."

Ranchers were also paid for not raising livestock. These programs were idiotic to logical and rational human beings.

Soon we had the Social Security Act implemented. People, yet alive in 2010, recall when the "government man" came to the place of employment to explain the plan. Workers were told emphatically that their social security number would NEVER be used under any circumstances for anything but their social security account!

The minimum wage law caused more unemployment. Punitive and unfair taxes were imposed, which were an impediment to economic growth.

The Works Project Administration (WPA) created government jobs proved to be no lasting solutions for the Great Depression. A standing joke asked the question: "What does WPA stand for?" The answer was, "We Piddle Around."

If a person worked for the WPA or the TVA, (Tennessee Valley Authority) a federally owned corporation in the United States created by congressional charter in May 1933 to provide navigation, flood control, electricity generation, fertilizer manufacturing, and economic development in the Tennessee River Valley area), they would have to become a Democrat and vote for Roosevelt if they wanted to keep their job.

Today because of the falling value of the dollar and the fear of super-inflation in the near future many people are turning to gold as a store of value. However, everyone needs to be reminded of what happened in 1933. President Franklin D. Roosevelt issued Executive Order #6102 on April 5, 1933. People holding gold coin or bullion were ordered to turn their gold over to the government in exchange for "paper" money. Failure to obey the order could result in a $10,000 fine ($166,640 in 2008 dollars) or up to ten years in prison or both.

According to syndicated columnist Dr. Walter Williams, the Soviet Union murdered about sixty-two million of its own people. In light of this fact how could Franklin Roosevelt refer to Joseph Stalin so warmly and kindly as "Uncle Joe"?

> ... when Congressman Martin Dies reported to the late President Franklin D. Roosevelt with a list of some 2,500 pro-communists, communists, agents, stooges, dupes, and witting or unwitting fellow travelers who were on the federal payroll and serving in key positions throughout the State Department, the Department of Justice, and the Department of Agriculture, the president replied angrily, "There is nothing wrong with

> communists. Some of the best friends I have are communists!"[17]

Moving on to the Truman administration, the United States government demonstrated great perfidy in its dealings with ardent anti-communist Chinese leader Chiang Kai-shek, (1887- 1975). President Truman sent over George C. Marshall to inform him that he must allow the Communist Chinese to immediately enter his government on a coalition basis. This Chiang Kai-shek would not do, so all aid was pulled and promises broken and 600,000,000 Chinese were betrayed into communist hands.

> When Marshall was sent to China with secret State Department orders, the Communists at that time were bottled up in two areas and were fighting a losing battle, but that because of those orders the situation was radically changed in favor of the Communists. Under those orders, as we know, Marshall embargoed all arms and ammunition to our allies in China. He forced the opening of the Nationalist-held Kalgan Mountain pass into Manchuria, to the end that the Chinese Communists gained access to the mountains of captured Japanese equipment. No need to tell the country about how Marshall tried to force Chiang Kai-shek to form a partnership government with the Communists.[18]

---

[17] Howard E. Kershner, *Dividing the Wealth,* Old Greenwich Connecticut: Devin-Adair Company, 146.

[18] McCarthy, Joe (1951). *Major Speeches and Debates.* pp.191, from speech of March 14, 1951. Reeves, Thomas C. *The Life and Times of Joe McCarthy.* pp. 371–374.

Years after this had occurred this writer was en route back to the United States after having fulfilled preaching engagements in Japan and South Korea. I stopped by way of Hong Kong. I bought more gifts there than I could possibly carry with me, so I had most of them shipped to my home city of Memphis, Tennessee. Later when I went to receive my shipment at the Memphis International Airport, the amount of duty charged was outrageous because, it was explained, the officials claimed that many of the items had originated in (at that time) economically boycotted "Red" China. The origin of my purchases was NOT Red China, but I had to pay the duty anyway. Later learning that our own socialistic nation had helped to create "Red" China added insult to injury! Not only did our politicians deceive the Chinese Nationalist Forces under Chiang Kai-shek, and deliver China over to the Communists who murdered some 60,000,000 innocent Chinese, we also handed over Rhodesia and South Africa into communistic and socialistic hands.

Once China had fallen, the hopes of Korea, Formosa, and Southeast Asia depended on the post-war commitments of the U. S. to protect them. But in January 1950, Dean Acheson announced that Korea, Formosa and the territory lying beyond were no longer within the "defense perimeter of the United States."

> Within six months, Russia launched an attack against little South Korea, using the Communists of North Korea as a façade. In all U.S. history, Americans had never fought a war as frustrating as the war in Korea. After a brilliant initial victory under astonishing odds, General Douglas MacArthur defeated and captured the North Korean army. He then began the mopping up process in North Korea and suddenly found his forces unexpectedly confronted by several hundred thousand "volunteer" Red Chinese. . . General MacArthur was not

even allowed to bomb the Yalu Bridge over which the Red Chinese were pouring their men and supplies. Nor was he allowed to attack the Chinese bases beyond the Yalu.[19]

After four months a congressman inquired of General MacArthur who had been muzzled and the whole truth was revealed. Within a few days after that Truman "fired" MacArthur and removed him from command. Our military was prevented from winning the Korean War. I interviewed two good friends of mine, Tom Lincoln and Jim Brown, who were officers in that war and they spoke of their annoyance with the lack of support in fighting the Chinese communists and trying to stay alive in forty degree below zero weather. My older brother was killed in action a few days after he turned twenty-one years of age. I never found real peace over this until twenty years later when I was preaching in South Korea and realized that it was his sacrifice and thousands of others like his that made this possible.

Carroll Quigley

DR. CARROLL QUIGLEY put out his *magnus opus* in 1966; an enormous one-volume history of the twentieth century entitled *Tragedy and Hope,* identifying the secret power structure that controls most of the governments of the world. According to Quigley, the *ESTABLISHMENT* is made up of the CFR (Council on Foreign Relations) and the International Bankers, the Institute of Pacific Relations, and the London-Wall Street axis and others. The *ESTABLISHMENT* is not for the communists, the socialists, the Democrats, the Republicans, or any one country—only for themselves and their best interests. According to Quigley, it was

---

[19] W. Cleon Skousen, *The Naked Capitalist*, 77.

the "Establishment" that put Woodrow Wilson in office as well as FDR, Truman, Kennedy, and Johnson. Quigley died early in January of 1977.

Although Quigley's conspiracy theory may seem to be a little far-fetched there are certain events in history that would be very difficult to fathom– unless he were right. However, some group with great power and influence had dissimilar plans for reasons unknown. If I understand Quigley correctly the Establishment is made up mostly of capitalists who believe global socialism is more advantageous to *them*.

Conspiracy theorist and conservative author Cleon Skousen (1913) reported that President Johnson by the suggestion of the *Communist Daily Worker,* appointed Earl Warren to head a commission to investigate the Kennedy assassination in his book *The Naked Capitalist* (Skousen, 99). Television news personality Glen Beck's attention to the writings of Skousen have resulted in a revival of interest in Skousen's ideas and books.

The Civil Rights movement was infested with communists. The Marxists had made a big mistake during the period of 1928-1934. When they tried to work in the Negro community with their anti-religious stand, "religion is the opiate of the people," they had alienated the Negro ministers. When they learned that among the lower and middle class, the Negro ministers were the leading force, they became silent regarding their anti-religious posture.

Martin Luther King, Jr. not only attended the communist training school Highlander Folk School of Monteagle, Tennessee, with Mrs. Rosa Parks and Ralph Abernathy, he surrounded himself with communists. Among his Marxists associates were Bayard Rustin, Stanley Levison, and Jack O'Dell. John F. Kennedy repeatedly warned King to stop associating himself with such subversives, but he never did.

King on Redistribution of Wealth

You can't talk about solving the economic problem of the Negro without talking about billions of dollars. You can't talk about ending the slums without first saying profit must be taken out of slums. You're really tampering and getting on dangerous ground because you are messing with folk then. You are messing with captains of industry... Now this means that we are treading in difficult water, because it really means that we are saying that something is wrong...with capitalism... There must be a better distribution of wealth and maybe America must move toward a Democratic Socialism. (*Myths of Martin Luther King, by* Marcus Epstein (<http://www.martinlutherkingbio.net/civil-rights-library/4-mlk/15-myths-of-martin-luther-king.html>)

President Bill Clinton tried to move us further down the socialist road with Hillary's socialized medicine scene but it failed to get passed. George W. Bush continued to increase the size of government and we wonder if his "compassionate conservative" could have been a code word for more socialism?

DEVELOPMENT OF LIBERALISM

CLASSIC LIBERALISM
MODERN LIBERALISM
PALEO-CONSERVATISM
NEO-CONSERVATISM

Legal scholar and historian William J. Novak wrote that *liberalism* in the United States made a swing, "between 1877 and 1937 from laissez-faire constitutionalism to New Deal statism, from classical liberalism to democratic social-welfarism."[20]

Classical liberalism is a political philosophy that arose in 19th century England, Western Europe, and the Americas. It commends the paradigm of limited government and liberty of individuals, freedom of religion, speech, press, assembly, and general concept of free markets.

Scottish economist Adam Smith (1723-1790) postulated that government should only be concerned with three major things: (1) protection against foreign invaders, (2) protection of citizens from wrongs committed against them by other citizens, and (3) building and maintaining public institutions and public works for the private sector did not have funds. Classical liberals extended protection of the country to protection of overseas markets through armed intervention.

In America, classical liberalism flourished because it had little resistance contrasted to Europe where it was opposed by many reactionary interests. In America, a nation of farmers, not much attention was paid to the economic features of classical liberalism. As the nation grew, industry became a larger part of American life. Classical liberalism stresses the sovereignty of the individual, with

---

[20] "The Not-So-Strange Birth of the Modern American State: A Comment on James A. Henretta's *Charles Evans Hughes and the Strange Death of Liberal America,*" Law and History Review 24, no. 1 (2006).

private property rights being seen as indispensable to individual liberty. The ideology of the original *classical liberals* argued against direct democracy "for there is nothing in the bare idea of majority rule to show that majorities will always respect the rights of property or maintain rule of law."[21]

Case in point, James Madison contended for a constitutional republic with safeguards for individual liberties, over a pure democracy, deducing that in a pure democracy, a "common passion or interest will, in almost every case, be felt by a majority of the whole...and there is nothing to check the inducements to sacrifice the weaker party...."[22]

It was in the term of Andrew Jackson that economic questions came to the vanguard. The economic ideas of the Jacksonian era were almost collectively the concepts of classical liberalism. The greatest extent of freedom was achieved when the government took a "hands off" approach toward industrial expansion and supported the value of the currency by backing paper money with gold.

The ideas of classical liberalism began to be questioned when a series of depressions occurred were thought to be impossible according to the doctrines of classical economics. Experiencing pecuniary hardship, voters demanded relief. William Jennings Bryan demonstrated outstanding oratorical skills when he made his renowned "Cross of Gold" speech July 9, 1896 at the Chicago

---

[21] Alan Ryan, "Liberalism", in *A Companion to Contemporary Political Philosophy*, ed. Robert E. Goodin and Philip Pettit (Oxford: Blackwell Publishing, 1995), 293.
[22] James Madison, Federalist No. 10 (November 22, 1787), in Alexander Hamilton, John Jay, and James Madison, *The Federalist: A Commentary on the Constitution of the United States*, ed. Henry Cabot Lodge (New York, 1888), 56.

Democratic National Convention, in which he made an appeal for bimetallism.[23]

"You shall not press down upon the brow of labor this crown of thorns, you shall not crucify mankind upon a cross of gold."

Classical liberalism was the standard principle of American businessmen until the Great Depression.[24] The Great Depression saw a alteration in liberalism, leading to the development of **modern liberalism**. In the words of Arthur Schlesinger Jr. "court historian" to John F. Kennedy:

> When the growing complexity of industrial conditions required increasing government intervention in order to assure more equal opportunities, the liberal tradition, faithful to the goal rather than to the dogma, altered its view of the state, and there emerged the conception of a social welfare state, in which the national government had the express obligation to maintain high levels of employment in the economy, to supervise standards of life and labor, to regulate the methods of business competition, and to establish comprehensive patterns of social security.[25]

---

[23] Following the Coinage Act (1873), the United States ended its policy of bimetallism and began to operate a *de facto* gold standard. In 1896, the Democratic Party wanted to standardize the value of the dollar to silver and opposed a monometallic gold standard. The inflation that would result from the silver standard would make it easier for farmers and others who had to live on credit for much of the year to pay off their debts by increasing their revenue dollars. It would also reverse the deflation which the U.S. experienced from 1873-1896.

[24] Eric Voegelin, Mary Algozin, and Keith Algozin, "Liberalism and Its History", *Review of Politics* 36, no. 4 (1974): 504-20.

[25] Arthur Schlesinger Jr., "Liberalism in America: A Note for Europeans", in *The Politics of Hope* (Boston: Riverside Press, 1962).

In Europe, especially, except in the British Isles, liberalism had been fairly weak and unpopular relative to its opposition, like socialism, and therefore no change in meaning occurred.[26]

By the late 1970s, however, stagnant economic growth and increased levels of taxation and debt spurred new ideas, sometimes called **conservatism** and sometimes called **classical liberalism**. The process of applying labels can often get one into hot water. Yet some form of terminology and categorization is necessary. The creeds of individuals are often complex and may not be easily sorted out.

More precisely and explicitly definitive, Conservatism must be sub-divided and includes several branches: Among them are: classical, core-value conservatism (Paleo-conservatism), the point of view to which this author subscribes; Classical Liberalism has become known today as Libertarianism, and Neo-Conservatism, supports using American economic and military power to bring democracy and human rights to other countries. In economics, unlike paleo-conservatives and libertarians, neo-conservatives are fairly comfortable with a welfare state. They are rhetorically supportive of free markets, but will intrude if they think it is in the best interest of the powers that be.

Economists Friedrich von Hayek and Milton Friedman argued against government intervention in fiscal policy and their ideas were embraced by conservative political parties in the US and the United Kingdom beginning in the 1980s.[27]

---

[26] Eric Voegelin, Mary Algozin, and Keith Algozin, "Liberalism and Its History," *Review of Politics* 36, no. 4 (1974): 504-20.
[27] *Encyclopædia Britannica Online*, s.v. "Liberalism" (by Harry K. Girvetz and Minogue Kenneth), p. 16 (accessed May 16, 2006).

Ronald Reagan credited Frederic Bastiat, Ludwig von Mises, and Hayek as influences.[28]

Most classic liberals would argue that free exchange of goods between nations will lead to a more peaceful world. French economist and free trade advocate Frederic Bastiat (1801-1850) said, "When goods cannot cross borders, armies will." Adam Smith predicted in the *Wealth of Nations* that as societies moved forward the spoils of war would rise, but the costs of war would rise, making war challenging and costly for industrialized nations.

British manufacturer and statesman Richard Cobden (1804-1865) said:

> ...the honours, the fame, the emoluments of war, belong not to [the middle and industrial classes]; the battle-plain is the harvest field of the aristocracy, watered with the blood of the people...Whilst our trade rested upon our foreign dependencies, as was the case in the middle of the last century . . . force and violence, were necessary to command our customers for our manufacturers. . . But war, although the greatest of consumers, not only produces nothing in return, but, by abstracting labour from productive employment and interrupting the course of trade, it impedes, in a variety of indirect ways, the creation of wealth; and, should hostilities be continued for a series of years, each successive war-loan will be felt in our commercial and manufacturing districts with an augmented pressure.[29]

Cobden thought that military spending exacerbated the wellbeing of the state and profited an elite minority. Cobden and many

---

[28] Ronald Reagan, "Insider Ronald Reagan: A Reason Interview", *Reason Magazine*, July 1975.
[29] Edward P. Stringham, "Commerce, Markets, and Peace: Richard Cobden's Enduring Lessons", *Independent Review* 9, no. 1 (2004): 105, 110, 115.

classical liberals believed those who advocated peace must also advocate free markets.

At the concept of "free trade," the various types of conservatives will cleave to different views.

From my point of view, we must not become a slave to principle or tradition. As a Southerner, traditionally I would be for free trade. But in today's world, I must modify my position. It should be obvious to anyone who has a grain of sense that American workers cannot compete with overseas slave labor without being reduced to their standard of living, and some protection of American labor is necessary.

It was stated at the beginning of this chapter that the ideas of classic liberalism were opposed by many reactionary interests in Europe and did not get a strong a foothold as they did in America. Curiously, while Britain was reveling in her great days as an empire under Queen Victoria, Fabianism and socialism were captivating the thoughts of some of her brightest minds.

One little group of brilliant but dissolute young people born in the late Victorian era had an unusual influence on the downward spiral of the social order as they rebelled against all probity and encouraged others to emulate their pattern.

The whole lot about them was *avant-garde*. They were the Bloomsbury Group, a group of writers, intellectuals, philosophers and artists who held informal discussions in the Bloomsbury district of London during the early part of the twentieth century. They viewed the capitalist system as obsolete. Just about everything in the established order they reviled. Same sex love affairs were pronounced as, "that love which passes all Christian understanding." These leftist degenerates proposed to secure public acceptance of their way-out ideas. Their work had a great impact on literature, the arts, and economics, as well as present-day attitudes towards feminism and sexuality. Somehow they managed to have quite an impact on the world. One of the most notable men in the was characterized by writer Zygmund Dobbs as the "gravedigger for the British empire." His name was John Maynard Keynes.

John Maynard Keynes

Quotes from John Maynard Keynes:
(1883-1946)
The best way to destroy the capitalist system is to debauch the currency. By a continuing process of inflation, governments can confiscate, secretly and unobserved, an important part of the wealth of their citizens.

By a continuous process of inflation, governments can confiscate, secretly and unobserved, an important part of the wealth of their citizens. By this method, they not only confiscate, but they confiscate arbitrarily; and while the process impoverishes many, it actually enriches some....The process engages all of the hidden forces of economic law on the side of destruction, and does it in a manner that not one man in a million can diagnose.
Economic Consequences of the Peace, 1920

I work for a Government I despise for ends I think criminal.

Perhaps one wonders why devote a chapter to the theories of a long dead economist who was characterized by his male sweetheart, Lytton Strachey, as "A liberal and a sodomite, an atheist and a statistician." Attention is called to him because we in the United States of America are living under the presidency of a man who thinks Keynesian economics is the answer to our problems in spite of the fact that they have proven to fail time after time in practice. We need to know more about the people who have influenced the president of the United States. We must to be wary of the character of everyone who has a hand in fomenting public policy, of those in influential positions. Would that England and the United States of America been more scrutinizing of John Maynard Keynes in the early part of the twentieth century and not given him a platform to spread his foolhardy and imprudent economic theories!

John Maynard Keynes (1883-1946) was the son of an English academic and had ample educational advantages. He was a radical thinker and an open bi-sexual whose his diary listed fifty gay affairs between the ages of eighteen and thirty-three.[30]

Keynesian economics theorizes that private sector choices may lead to ineffective macroeconomic results supports much involvement from the public quarter. This would include monetary policy actions by a central bank and of the government to try to make business cycles more stable.[31] The theories that shape the foundation of Keynesian economics were first given in *The General Theory of Employment, Interest and Money,* 1936. The book, made popular fiscal "fine-tuning" or the idea that more **government spending will cause an economy to accelerate by a stimulus.** He also theorized that a fiscal contraction will slow things down. A little adjustment on the fiscal "machine" is supposedly all that is needed to "fix" demand so that it matches an economy's capability to increase productivity.

Keynes promoted a mixed economy, chiefly private sector, but with a large role of government and public sector. This was the economic model during the latter part of the Great Depression, World War II, and the post-war economic expansion (1945–1973). We should have learned the lessons of Keynesian economics,

---

[30] (http://www.thisislondon.co.uk/standard/article-23575559-ten-things-you-didnt-know-about-mr-keynes.do)
[31] Sullivan, Arthur; Steven M. Sheffrin (2003). *Economics: Principles in action.* Upper Saddle River: Pearson Prentice Hall.

which brought us stagflation in the 1970s and trillions of dollars of debt.

The former British Prime Minister Gordon Brown and Richard Nixon, who claimed that he was not particularly a fan of big government, used Keynesian economics to validate government stimulus programs for their economies. On August 15, 1971, President Richard M. Nixon took the U.S. completely off the gold standard. In 1971, Nixon announced, "We are all Keynesians now."[32]

It was a tidy hypothesis, and it enthralled two generations of economists, especially those who were fond of a strong central government concept. When Margaret Thatcher became British prime minister in 1981, Britain's fiscal deficit was a large 5.6% of the gross domestic product, and the economy was in the middle of a slump. To revive the economy, Thatcher set up a tight fiscal squeeze in addition to a expansionary monetary policy. This was instantaneously and heartily denounced by 364 dedicated Keynesian economists. In a letter to the London *Times* they predicted, "Present policies will deepen the depression, erode the industrial base of our economy and threaten its social and political stability."[33] But Mrs. Thatcher was quickly proven correct. Soon after this dire forecast, the economy turned around and boomed for the next five years. The consequence was utter astonishment among the Keynesian devotees.

Although Keynes made public statements that he was not a communist, there is abundant evidence that he certainly did not

---

[32] (Daniel Yergin and Joseph Stanislaw, *The Commanding Heights*, 1997, ed., pages 60-64)
[33] (http://members.forbes.com/global/1999/0222/0204077a.html)

think highly of capitalism. Many scholars consider him to have liked the ideas of communism *in theory,* but *in practice* he enjoyed his hedonistic lifestyle and his status as an eminent British economist.

John Maynard Keynes held communism in high regard. In June 1936, on a BBC radio program entitled "Books and Authors," Keynes commented on Sidney and Beatrice Webb's *Soviet Communism: A New Civilization.* Here is what he said:

> Until recently events in Russia were moving too fast and the gap between paper professions and actual achievements was too wide for a proper account to be possible. But the new system is now sufficiently crystallized to be reviewed. The result is impressive. The Russian innovators have passed, not only from the revolutionary stage, but also from the doctrinaire stage. There is little or nothing left bears any special relation to Marx and Marxism as distinguished from other systems of socialism. They are engaged in the vast administrative task of making a completely new set of social and economic institutions work smoothly and successfully over a territory so extensive that it covers one-sixth of the land surface of the world. Methods are still changing rapidly in response to experience. The largest scale empiricism and experimentalism which has ever been attempted by disinterested administrators is in operation.[34]

---

[34] Keynes, John Maynard. Elizabeth Johnson and Donald Moggridge, eds. *The Collected Writings of John Maynard Keynes.* Cambridge: Cambridge University Press, 1982. 28:333-334.

Keynes also hoped for the same social experiment to be conducted in Britain:

> It leaves me with a strong desire and hope that we in this country may discover how to combine an unlimited readiness to experiment with changes in political and economic methods and institutions, whilst preserving traditionalism and a sort of careful conservatism, thrifty of everything has human experience behind it, in every branch of feeling and of action.[35]

(http://www.believeallthings.com/1472/john-maynard-keynes-communism/)

One would think the out-dated economic theories of a degenerate like John Maynard Keynes would have been long forgotten, but they have been revived by Barack Obama, whose liberal entourage parallels Bloomsbury group.

> Roosevelt's Keynesian economics was left for dead in the 1980s with President Reagan's supply-side revolution miraculously ending the stagflation of the 1970s with a 25-year economic boom. But President Obama came into office talking as if that never happened, casting it down the memory hole. While Reagan's early 1981 budget cuts slashed the federal budget by about 5%, Obama rammed through an almost $1 trillion stimulus package of nearly all Keynesian economics from the 1930s, laughing at his astounded critics with the question, "What do you think a stimulus is?"
>
> **Economically, it didn't work, just as it didn't in the 1930s or the 1970s. Now 29 months after the**

---

[35] Ibid.

recession officially started in December, 2007, unemployment is 10% and rising, and the stock market is again stumbling, with the Dow still 4000 points off its last highs. The recovery was overdue a year ago, and even now economic growth is not half what it should be.

But note how the stimulus spending was structured so that more is spent this year than last. Was the goal to reduce unemployment as quickly as possible, or to use the guise of Keynesian stimulus spending for a political slush fund to buy as many votes as possible in this political year? Note also that about half of the direct "stimulus" spending went to state and local governments to prop up the employment of public employees, the most reliable supporters of liberal Democrat candidates. The only thing President Obama's stimulus is stimulating is a left-wing Democrat political machine.[36]

---

[36] (http://spectator.org/archives/2010/05/26/what-barack-obama-is-thinking)

Barack Obama: the Result

Now we come to a full blown socialist in President Barack Hussein Obama. He is even called a socialist by the neo-conservatives as well as by the paleo-conservatives. Is it really fair to call Obama a socialist?

Well, when I see an animal that looks like a polar bear, smells like a polar bear, walks like a polar bear, growls like a polar bear, associates with polar bears, and is in danger of extinction, I must assume that it is indeed a polar bear.

Anyone with a clear and open mind will have no problem acknowledging that Barack Hussein Obama is a true and dedicated socialist.

A Harris Poll released Wednesday, March 24, 2010, found that 40 percent of Americans say Mr. Obama is a socialist, and a third think he's a Muslim, and a "domestic enemy that the U. S. Constitution speaks of."

Blogger "Chris of Rights" was frightfully accurate when he made the following prognostications comparing Obama to a Marxist back in 2008.

Posted by Chris of Rights at 8:34 AM, June 6, 2008

> Recently, someone called me deluded for having the temerity to suggest that Barack Obama (D-IL) has Marxist/socialistic views.
>
> Actually, he said that I claimed he was a Marxist (I didn't) and that delusion was putting it mildly. Unfortunately, I took the bait offered and then did call Obama a Marxist.

I'll go back now to saying that he has Marxist/socialistic views and agenda.

And I'll spend the rest of this very long post backing that up. I'm going to talk about a lot of things here, and I really should break it up into several posts, but I'm not going to.

Let's start by looking at some of his history:

1. Obama says that the well-known Marxist, Frank Marshall Davis was a "decisive influence" on him. This is in his book and has been documented by the Communist Party USA.

2. Obama says, "All of my life, I carried a single image of my father, one that I tried to take as my own." But what do we know about his father? We know that he supported:

> 100% taxation
>
> communal farms / the elimination of private farming
>
> the nationalization of businesses owned by "Europeans" and "Asians".
>
> "active" measures to bring about a classless society
>
> Obama cites as one of his mentors and friends, the now infamous Bill Ayers, well known Marxist and terrorist.
>
> Obama's (until recent) church of twenty years is the Trinity United Church of Chicago. The Trinity United Church openly teaches Black Liberation Theology. Thousands have articles have been written documenting the ties between **Black Liberation Theology and Marxism**. It literally has its origins there.

3. When running for state senate in 1996, Barack Obama obtained the endorsement of the Democratic Socialists of America. In case you don't know who they are, I'll quote from their website: "The Democratic Socialists of America (DSA) is the largest socialist organization in the United States, and the principal U.S. affiliate of the Socialist International. DSA's members are building progressive movements for social change while establishing an openly socialist presence in American communities and politics." (I have originally stated that he sought this endorsement--I was confusing them with the New Party--see below). It's not as if this group just automatically supports Illinois Democrats. They only supported 4 that year.

4. When running for state senate in 1996, Barack Obama sought and obtained the endorsement of the New Party. There are conflicting statements as to whether or not this was Barack Obama's first political party. If you don't know who the New Party is, that's because they are now defunct. But, like a phoenix, they have risen from the ashes as ACORN.

Ok, that's all guilt by association, but it makes it quite plain that many of the people in Obama's inner circle, the people that inspired Obama, and the people that have supported Obama, are Marxist or at least have Marxist leanings.

Let's look at some of Obama's statements:

> Well, Charlie, what I've said is that I would look at raising the capital gains tax for purposes of fairness.
>
> This is despite the empirical evidence and even statements by members of his own party, that raising the capital gains tax *reduces government revenue*. He doesn't care how much the government brings in as long as taxes are "fair."

And it's not surprising then they get bitter, they cling to guns or religion.

Compare to "Religion is the opiate of the masses," Karl Marx, 1843

Each of you will have the chance to make your own discovery in the years to come. And I say "chance" because you won't have to take it. There's no community service requirement in the real world; no one forcing you to care. You can take your diploma, walk off this stage, and chase only after the big house and the nice suits and all the other things that our money culture says you should buy. You can choose to narrow your concerns and live your life in a way that tries to keep your story separate from America's. But I hope you don't. Not because you have an obligation to those who are less fortunate, though you do have that obligation. Not because you have a debt to all those who helped you get here, though you do have that debt. It's because you have an obligation to yourself. Because our individual salvation depends on collective salvation. Because thinking only about yourself, fulfilling your immediate wants and needs, betrays a poverty of ambition. Because it's only when you hitch your wagon to something larger than yourself that you realize your true potential and discover the role you'll play in writing the next great chapter in America's story.

Those are pretty words, and somehow uplifting in the "it takes a village" meme of uplifting, but the translation is simple. "Put away your childish thoughts of the American Dream. Serve the larger community. Share with the larger community." Community is a big word in socialism.

I've read that there are at least 15 complimentary references to Che Guevara on Obama's own website. Certainly Che is no friend to capitalism (or freedom), but without a link, I suggest you decide on your own the worthiness of this statement.

Ok, there's no smoking gun statement there. You have to read between the lines. What? You are expecting him to just come out and say "I am a Marxist and I want to turn the country into a socialist state?"

First of all, I don't think he thinks of himself as a Marxist/socialist (and I've tried very hard myself not to call him that, but instead to say that has a Marxist/socialist agenda). And second, even if he did, that's clearly not the way to get elected.)

Ok, let's now look at his **"Blueprint for Change,"** or as I like to call it, his **"Blueprint for Socialism."**

Before I begin in depth, here's the Webster definition of **socialism**:

1: any of various economic and political theories advocating collective or governmental ownership and administration of the means of production and distribution of goods.

2: a system of society or group living in there is no private property or a system or condition of society in the means of production are owned and controlled by the state.

3: a stage of society in Marxist theory transitional between capitalism and communism and distinguished by unequal distribution of goods and pay according to work done.

The last definition there is interesting. Let's see what Webster has to say about **capitalism**:

an economic system characterized by private or corporate ownership of **capital** goods, by investments that are determined by private decision, and by prices, production, and the distribution of goods that are determined mainly by competition in a free market.

and **communism**:

1 **a:** a theory advocating elimination of private property **b:** a system in goods are owned in common and are available to all as needed.

2 *capitalized* **a:** a doctrine based on revolutionary Marxian socialism and Marxism-Leninism that was the official ideology of the Union of Soviet Socialist Republics **b:** a totalitarian system of government in a single authoritarian party controls state-owned means of production **c:** a final stage of society in Marxist theory in the state has withered away and economic goods are distributed equitably **d: communist** systems collectively.

Also, under socialism Webster defines **state socialism** as:

an economic system with limited socialist characteristics that is effected by gradual state action and typically includes public ownership of major industries and remedial measures to benefit the working class.

and **Marxism** is defined this way:

the political, economic, and social principles and policies advocated by Marx; *especially* **:** a theory and practice of socialism including the labor theory of value, dialectical materialism, the class struggle, and dictatorship of the proletariat until the establishment of a classless society.

And what about **proletariat**?

1: the laboring class; *especially* **:** the class of industrial workers who lack their own means of production and hence sell their labor to live.

2: the lowest social or economic class of a community.

Ok, so basically, Marxism is a socialism that grants more and more power to the working class in order to achieve a classless society, and does this through the policies advocated by Marx, and socialism is an economic system that does not have private or corporate goods, does not have investments determined by private decision and does not have prices, production and distribution of goods determined by the free market. It also does have goods owned in common and available to all as needed, and included public ownership of major industries and remedial measures to benefit the working class.

And, as a reminder, **the 10 Planks of the Communist Manifesto**.

1. Abolition of **property in land** and application of all **rents** of land to public purposes.
2. A heavy progressive or graduated income tax.
3. Abolition of all right of inheritance.
4. Confiscation of the property of all **emigrants** and **rebels.**
5. Centralization of **credit** in the hands of the **State**, by means of a **national bank** with State **capital** and an exclusive **monopoly**.
6. Centralization of the means of **communication** and **transport** in the hands of the State.

7. Extension of **factories** and **instruments of production** owned by the State; the bringing into **cultivation** of **waste-lands**, and the improvement of the **soil** generally in accordance with a **common plan**.
8. Equal **liability** of all to labour. Establishment of industrial **armies**, especially for **agriculture**.
9. Combination of agriculture with **manufacturing industries**; gradual abolition of the distinction between **town** and **country**, by a more equable **distribution of the population** over the country.
10. **Free education** for all children in **public schools**. Combination of education with industrial production, &c., &c.[4]

Or, to sum up, as Marx himself did: "A sympathy for the working class or proletariat and a belief that the ultimate interests of workers best match those of humanity in general."

Where does Obama's Blueprint stack up?

1. Abolition of private ownership of land. I don't see anything on this, so I think Karl would give Obama a thumbs down. However, Obama has remained completely silent on the Kelo decision by the SCOTUS, and has in fact, praised the Justices on the majority side of this opinion. He's also made use of "eminent domain" in the web to take over a MySpace site devoted to him.

2. A heavily progressive income tax:

    Obama will restore fairness to the tax code and provide 150 million workers the tax relief they need. Obama will create a new "Making Work Pay" tax credit of up to $500 per person, or $1,000 per working family. The "Making Work Pay" tax credit will completely eliminate income taxes for 10 million Americans.

Obama will reform the Child and Dependent Care Tax Credit by making it refundable and allowing low-income families to receive up to a 50 percent credit for their child care expenses.

Obama supports increasing the maximum amount of earnings covered by Social Security.

Obama will eliminate all income taxation of seniors making less than $50,000 per year. Obama is committed to repealing the Bush tax cuts for the wealthiest Americans. Obama will cut income taxes by $1,000 for working families to offset the payroll tax they pay.

I'd say Obama gets a big thumbs up from Karl Marx on his tax positions. Notice especially there's a lot of the phrases "working families" and "wealthiest Americans." Creating class envy is a first step in working towards a classless society. And I think Marx would accept working families" in place of his "proletariat."

2. Abolition of all rights to inheritance. Well, I don't see anything in his "Blueprint for Change" about this, but I also don't see anything about reducing or eliminating the inheritance tax. Karl would want Obama to go father here, but you can definitely say that Obama's not moving any farther away from Marxism on this one.
3. Confiscation of property of emigrants and rebels Obama gets a big thumbs down from Karl.
4. **National Bank**. We're already there. Nothing more for Obama to do here.
5. Centralization of communication and transport.

Obama will encourage the deployment of the most modern communications infrastructure.

Karl would be proud. Note that there are a lot of subtleties here. When a politician uses phrases like "will encourage," "should not be allowed," "will prevent," "will ensure," and he's talking about businesses, he's talking about more government control over business, is exactly the opposite of letting the free market decide things and is precisely in line with moving towards a socialistic environment.

6. Extension of state-owned factories and improvement of the soil in accordance with a *common* plan.

Barack Obama will prevent companies from abusing their monopoly power through unjustified price increases.

Obama supports implementation of a market-based cap-and-trade system to reduce carbon emissions by the amount scientists say is necessary: 80 percent below 1990 levels by 2050. Obama's cap-and-trade system will require all pollution credits to be auctioned.

Obama will create a Global Energy Forum that includes all G-8 members plus Brazil, China, India, Mexico and South Africa— the largest energy consuming nations from both the developed and developing world. The forum would focus exclusively on global energy and environmental issues.

The UNFCCC process is the main international forum dedicated to addressing the climate problem and an Obama administration will work constructively within it.

Obama will increase incentives for farmers and private landowners to conduct sustainable agriculture and protect wetlands, grasslands, and forests.

Once again, the tendency here is away from the free market, and definitely moves towards improvement of the soil through a common plan. If Karl were alive today he'd be up on his feet for Obama by now.

7. Establishment of industrial armies, especially for agriculture.

Obama will strengthen the ability of workers to organize unions. He will fight for passage of the Employee Free Choice Act. Obama will ensure that his labor appointees support workers' rights and will work to ban the permanent replacement of striking workers. Obama will ensure our farm programs help family farmers, not giant corporations.

Obama will fight for farm programs that provide family farmers with stability and predictability. Obama supports guaranteeing workers seven paid sick days per year.

There's not much that's big here, but let's face it, industrial armies have long been the goal of the Democratic party. Obama may not bring much new to the table here, but he doesn't move any farther away from Marx either.

8. Gradual abolition of the distinction between town and country. To be honest, I'm not sure what this means, and I'm not sure that Marx would write it quite this way if he were writing today (remember all of his stuff was done before the industrial revolution) however:

Obama will invest in rural small businesses and fight to expand high-speed Internet access. He will improve rural schools and attract more doctors to rural areas!

Barack Obama will ensure that rural Americans have access to a modern communications infrastructure. He will modernize an FCC program that supports rural phone service so that it promotes affordable broadband coverage across rural America as well.

Rural health care providers often get less money from Medicare and Medicaid for the very same procedure performed in urban areas. Obama will work to ensure a more equitable Medicare and Medicaid reimbursement structure. He will attract providers to rural America by creating a loan forgiveness program for doctors and nurses who work in underserved rural areas. He supports increasing rural access to care by promoting health information technologies like telemedicine. Obama will create a Rural Revitalization Program to attract and retain young people to rural America. Obama will increase research and educational funding for Land Grant colleges. Obama will invest in the core infrastructure, roads, bridges, locks, dams, water systems and essential air service that rural communities need.

I think it's safe to say that Karl would still be pleased. If we go back to our definition of socialism, we see a lot of goods being made available to all as needed.

9. Free education for all children in public schools.

Obama will expand the Youth Build program, gives disadvantaged young people the chance to complete their high school education, learn valuable skills and build affordable housing in their communities. He will grow the program so that 50,000 low-income young people a year a chance to learn construction job skills and complete high school.

Obama believes that the goal of No Child Left Behind was the right one, but that it was written and implemented poorly and it has demoralized our educators and broken its promise to our children. Obama will fund No Child Left Behind and improve its assessments and accountability systems.

Obama will create a new American Opportunity Tax Credit that will make tuition at the nation's community colleges completely free.

Obama will double funding for the main federal support for afterschool programs, the 21st Century Learning Centers program, to serve one million more children.

Obama's "STEP UP" plan addresses the achievement gap by supporting summer learning opportunities for disadvantaged children through partnerships between local schools and community organizations.

Obama supports outreach programs like GEAR UP, TRIO and Upward Bound to encourage more young people from low-income families to consider and prepare for college.

There's little doubt that if Karl were alive now, he'd be standing up and cheering for Obama.

And here's some more pieces that I think obviously qualify as socialist in nature, but I can't find a place in the 10 planks where they easily fit.

Obama will make available a new national health plan so all Americans, including the self-employed and small businesses, can buy affordable health coverage that is similar to the plan available to members of Congress.

The Obama Plan will have the Following Features:

Guaranteed Eligibility: No American will be turned away FROM ANY INSURANCE PLAN because of illness or pre-existing conditions.

Comprehensive Benefits: The benefit package will be similar to that offered through Federal Employees Health Benefits Program (FEHBP), the plan members of Congress have. The plan will cover all essential medical services, including preventive, maternity and mental health care.

Affordable Premiums, Co-Pays and Deductibles.

The Obama plan will create a National Health Insurance Exchange to help individuals who wish to purchase a private insurance plan. The Exchange will act as a watchdog group and help reform the private insurance market by creating rules and standards for participating insurance plans to ensure fairness and to make individual coverage more affordable and accessible.

Employers that do not offer or make a meaningful contribution to the cost of quality health coverage for their employees will be required to contribute a percentage of payroll toward the costs of the national plan. Obama will require that all children have health care coverage.

Obama will set a goal that all middle and high school students do 50 hours of community service a year. He will develop national guidelines for service-learning and will give schools better tools both to develop programs and to document student experience.

Obama will establish a new American Opportunity Tax Credit that worth $4,000 a year in exchange for 100 hours of *public* service a year.

Obama will ensure that at least 25 percent of College Work-Study funds are used to support *public* service opportunities instead of jobs in dining halls and libraries.

And, as one last reminder, our earlier definitions of Marxism and socialism:

> Marxism is a socialism that grants more and more power to the working class in order to achieve a classless society, and does this through the policies advocated by Marx, and socialism is an economic system that does not have private or corporate goods, does not have investments determined by private decision and does not have prices, production and distribution of goods determined by the free market.
>
> All the quoted pieces above are from his PLAN sections of the Blueprint. There are even more examples of his socialistic views in his RECORD sections.
>
> I highly suggest you read the **entire document**.
>
> Your Honor, ladies and gentlemen of the jury, the prosecution rests.
>
> (<http://chrisofrights.blogspot.com/2008/06/barack-obama-and-socialismmarxism.html>)

To add to our problems we have perhaps the most corrupt and dim Congress since the times of Lincoln and Grant.

During the Roosevelt administration we had a number of famous, (or was it infamous) bank robbers in history, although they were little threat at all to the general public. One well known outlaw was Charles Arthur, "Pretty Boy" Floyd (1904-1934). Woodie Guthrie wrote the *Ballad of Pretty Boy Floyd,* who was reported as saying, "some rob with a six gun, others with a fountain pen." I am not defending Pretty Boy, but I must say truer words were never spoken.

We have a Congress that gives themselves a raise while reducing the social security checks for millions of Americans.

There were a pair of "public enemies" known as "Bonnie and Clyde," Bonnie Parker (1910-1934) and Clyde Barrow (1909-

1934). Today, we have a pair of public enemies that are ten thousand times more dangerous. They are "Nancy and Harry."

We also have the most dangerous president since Abraham Lincoln. Not only is Obama a Marxist in public speech throughout his political career, he has flip-flopped on the subject of Reparations. Even Neo-Conservative Rush Limbaugh criticized Obama's ideas about reparations:

> As the economy performs worse than expected, the deficit for the 2010 budget year beginning in October will worsen by $87 billion to $1.3 trillion. The deterioration reflects lower tax revenues and higher costs for bank failures, unemployment benefits and food stamps. But in the Oval Office of the White House none of this is a problem. This is the objective. The objective is unemployment. The objective is more food stamp benefits. The objective is more unemployment benefits. The objective is an expanding welfare state. And the objective is to take the nation's wealth and return to it to the nation's quote, "rightful owners." Think reparations. Think forced reparations here if you want to understand what actually is going on. (<http://www.brendan-nyhan.com/blog/2009/05/limbaugh-claims-obama-supports-reparations.html >)

Others have also spoken out *a propos* Obama's view toward reparations.

> While he was an Illinois state senator, Barack Obama told a Chicago radio show host that he sought "major redistributive change" for the benefit of fellow blacks.
>
> He was speaking in the context of the civil rights movement, and how it had fallen short of "economic

justice." Although John McCain and other Republicans are afraid to say it, his remarks can only be interpreted to mean one thing: economic reparations for slavery. This is yet another example of Obama's lack of candor and deception about his true radical agenda during this campaign, as well as the mainstream media's failure to vet such serious issues and force them out into the open where voters can see them and have a fair chance to evaluate them before they go to the polls. In 2001, Obama said it's a "tragedy" the Constitution wasn't radically interpreted to force redistribution of wealth for blacks, and it's still an issue of concern for him today. And he suggested he wants to effect "major redistributive change" through legislation. He complained that during the civil-rights era, "the Supreme Court never ventured into issues of redistribution of wealth" for blacks, and that the Warren Court was not "radical" enough. "One of the tragedies of the civil-rights movement was there was a tendency to lose track of the political and community organizing activities on the ground that are able to put together the actual coalitions of power through you bring about redistributive change," he said while serving as a state lawmaker and University of Chicago lecturer. "And in some ways, we still suffer from that."

... in other words, stealth reparations. He says government should offer "universal" programs -- such as universal health care, universal mortgage credits, college tuition, job training and even universal 401(k)s -- that "disproportionately affect people of color." Obama's 2006 book and Web site outline a plan calling for essentially a government bailout of the inner cities, he describes as "repositories for all the scars of slavery and violence of Jim Crow." Among other things, he proposes:

- Doling out federal grants "targeting ex-offenders or substance abusers;"
- Subsidizing supermarket chains that relocate to the inner city;
- Creating a "universal 401(k)" in which the government would tax private contributions and match public contributions made into new retirement accounts by low-income families;
- Imposing "goals and timetables for minority hiring" on large corporations whose work forces are deemed too white;
- Ramping up funding for the Community Development Block Grant program, Head Start and HUD public housing subsidies.
- Funding Small Business Administration loans for minority; businesses who train ex-felons, including gangbangers, for the "green jobs" of the future, such as installing extra insulation in homes;
- Doubling the funding for federal after-school programs such as midnight basketball;
- Subsidizing job training, day care, transportation for inner-city poor, as well as doubling the funding of the federal Jobs Access and Reverse Commute program;
- Expanding the eligibility of the earned income tax credit to include more poor, and indexing it to inflation;
- Adopting entire inner-city neighborhoods as wards of the federal government; and
- Spending billions on new inner-city employment programs, including prison-to-work programs.

Claiming "blacks were forced into ghettos," Obama is certainly sympathetic to the idea of reparations. His church has actively petitioned for them for decades. And he's strongly suggested there's a legal case to be made for them.

In calling for a "new order," he invoked the memory of ABOLITIONISTS and their "willingness to spill blood and not just words ... that helped force the issue of a nation half slave and half free."

(by Sperry Hoover, Frontpagemag.com October 28, 2008 http://97.74.65.51/readArticle.aspx?ARTID=32892)

Summary of Newsmax.com Article on Reparations

Sunday, February 21, 2010, Newsmax.com reported that Obama has agreed to a plan to give $1.25 billion dollars in reparations to black farmers for claimed racial discrimination experienced under the Department of Agriculture's loan programs. Obama announced the arrangement on Thursday, and congratulated Agriculture Secretary Tom Vilsack and Attorney General Eric Holder for "bringing these long-ignored claims of African American farmers to a rightful conclusion."

The Washington Post reported that the payment was "part of a wider effort by Obama and senior officials to dispense with lawsuits stemming from America's checkered civil rights legacy."

House Majority Whip and Congressional Black Caucus member James Clyburn in expressing approval said, "History has taught us to never give up when fighting for what is right. What happened to these black farmers was wrong, and we now have the opportunity to make it right."

Clyburn said, "I thank President Obama for his leadership on this issue. I especially want to congratulate my colleagues in the Congressional Black Caucus for keeping the focus on the plight of black farmers."

However, Congress, in addition to a federal judge, must now approve the deal. The Justice Department informed the *Washington Post* that claims up to $50,000 may be made to the federal government through an relatively simple procedure, while larger claims will involve more detail in the substantiation of government discrimination that a "victim" gives. The charges made by thousands of black farmers, with blameworthiness at last acknowledged by Washington, accuse the USDA of decades of "racist practices." The $1.25 billion is only a portion, however, of the amount of money that the reparations movement has asked for to recompense for all the so called "unfair treatment of blacks in American history."

Some years ago the National Legal and Policy Center studied slave reparations activism and found some supporters want the federal government "to pay $500,000 to every slave descendant," which would total "more than $15 trillion and require a surtax of roughly $50,000 on each non-African American man, woman and child in this country (the median family income is not even that high)."

In his book, *The Debt: What America Owes to Blacks*, TransAfrica founder Randall Robinson, contended that "Solutions must be tailored to the scope of the crime in a way that would make the victim whole. In this case, the psychic and economic injury is enormous, multidimensional and long-running. Thus must be America's restitution to blacks for the damage done."

When we examine the entitlement mindset of the reparations folks, President Obama's $1.25 billion for 70,000-plus black farmers is scarcely a beginning.[37]

---

[37] (http://www.newsmax.com/Newsfront/obama-reparations-black-farmers/2010/02/21/id/350458)

SOCIALISM AND PROPERTY

A. By the Property Tax and Eminent Domain

The socialist agenda is to end the private ownership of property. They wanted to see common property of the whole society. To them private ownership is unacceptable and not allowed.

Thomas Jefferson believed that a tax on income could be legitimate but was strongly opposed to a property tax. He was of the opinion that one should not have to rent (through taxes) his own house from the state.

One of the goals of socialism is the redistribution of wealth. Before property or wealth can be redistributed it must first be confiscated (stolen) from someone else.

Today in the United States there is in reality no such thing as home ownership.

> The concept of the property tax is ultimately the idea that the state really owns all property and that you have the use of it only as long as you pay your yearly fee for its use. Fail to do so, and the real owner will soon claim "your" property, and you will be forced to move on, only to repeat the same scenario somewhere else unless you choose to rent instead of to buy. (Kennedy and Benson, 178)

John Swett was the state superintendent of schools in California from 1863 to 1868. According to Swett:

> The property of the state should be taxed to educate the children of the state. Notice Swett's language, very often repeated, the property *of the state*, not the property *in the*

state, and the children *of the state,* not the children *residing in the territory of the states.* (R. J. Rushdoony, *Messianic Character of American Education,* 79)

Chief Justice John Marshall said, "On unlimited powers to tax involves, necessity, a power to destroy; because there is a limit beyond no institution and no property can bear taxation."

In 1860 Mississippi was the richest state in the Union. After the War for Southern Independence the slaves, which represented great wealth, were lost without compensation. Slightly over 49% of households in Mississippi owned slaves. In 1867 an additional tax of $15.00 on each bale of cotton was devastating and gave India and Egypt control of the world cotton market.

According to Andrew Grayson in the pamphlet, *The Black Death* the property tax in Mississippi was fourteen times higher in 1874 than in 1873. In that one year 7,000,000 acres of land were forfeited.

The highly regarded historian, Thomas A. Bailey, in *The American Pageant,* reported:

> Burdensome taxes were passed in Mississippi, where some 6,000,000 acres were sold for delinquent taxes. The disfranchised and propertied white had to stagger along under a tax burden that sometimes rose ten or fifteen-fold. [This was but another glorious instance of taxation without representation.]

Many will say that what happened in the South is of little concern to the rest of the nation and is not relevant today. This is a foolish notion when one comes to the understanding that the state already owns our property and we have a socialist president who believes in the redistribution of wealth.

The fact of eminent domain also proves that the state has power over all property. R. J. Rushdoony, in his book, *Politics of Guilt and Pity*, expresses the danger of the right of eminent domain.

> In Biblical law, the state has no right of eminent domain and no right to tax the land. It is impossible to dispossess men of this inheritance under the law of the Lord as no taxes were levied against the land. The state was limited to a tax on increase, not on the land itself. The marks of a tyrant and a supplanter of God's kingship over a people was specified as oppressive taxation, and the confiscation of land by eminent domain. (**I Samuel: 8**). The state in claiming eminent domain, is simply asserting sovereign power over all the property within the state. The right of eminent domain ostensibly limits the state to the confiscation of properties necessary to the common good, or to the public welfare. But the state is the judge of the common good and public welfare, and as the power of eminent domain expands steadily towards the total possession by the state of all properties within the state. (326)

The presupposition therefore of the socialist will view private ownership as adverse to the common good, whereas state ownership is an advancement of the public welfare.

B. BY A GRADUATED INCOME TAX

The graduated or progressive income tax is a tax that is leveled on income. A level percentage of tax on income would result in those with higher income paying more in taxes. However, with the graduated income tax the higher incomes are taxed at higher percentage penalizes those who are prudent and successful.

The first graduated income tax, as we have seen, was initiated by Abraham Lincoln during his aggressive war against the Southern Confederate states. The unpopular tax was finally ruled unconstitutional by the Supreme Court in 1895. Under President Woodrow Wilson, the graduated income tax was again put into force in 1913. This time, however, it was made secure by the 16th amendment to the constitution, which legalized the income tax.

Employers were burdened by withdrawal tax on wages and filing reports is awesome. Some have defined slavery as involuntary servitude. Under this definition we all have become slaves to the government.

Mrs. Roper and I had the pleasant experience of living for a short time in the Cayman Islands. Most goods there are imported and an import tax from 20 to 27% is paid before the goods clear customs. The whole government operates on this simple tax. No income tax, no property tax, no sales tax, no estate tax, and NO RECORDS to keep or reports to be filled out.

While we were in the Cayman Islands we became acquainted with a contractor from Arkansas. He had been in the Caymans for eight years and had obtained Caymanian status. I asked him if he ever intended to return to the states and he replied, "No. I might visit there, but I like it here. I always hated keeping records and filling out forms. The only records I keep now are on the back of a paper sack and when I make a buck, I stick it in my pocket, and it is mine."

Our present income tax is unfair, stifles incentive, and requires many hours of paperwork. The time spent by individuals and government agencies could be used in a more productive manner.

C. BY ESTATE AND INHERITANCE TAX

"A good man leaveth an inheritance to his children's children."
Proverbs 13:22

Today our socialistic government believes that the inheritance belongs to them to redistribute as they see fit. Since the children did not earn the money or property left by the parents, and anti-Christian government claims the right to confiscate the wealth and use it to buy votes whereby the corrupt politicians can stay in office with great power.

Upon returning from the Cayman Islands in the early 1980s, I worked for a while with Aetna Life Insurance calling upon farmers with Estate tax problems. Farms, as well as small businesses, were being lost by the legitimate heirs because of an unfair and unscriptural estate tax. The federal government demanded 70% at that time of the total worth of the deceased. They did not want hogs or cattle or tractors, they wanted <u>cash</u> within nine months. As a result, the heirs were losing farms that had been in the family for years. President Reagan did manage to get the tax rate down to 55%. The future of this tax, although forgiven in the year 2010 returns, in 2011 and under our present socialistic administration, does not look good. Many *states* additionally claim an inheritance tax.

The creation of a welfare state or socialistic society would be virtually impossible without a National Bank (Federal Reserve System), fiat money, and confiscation of wealth.

Prior to 1911 when hard times came, families took care of families, churches took care of their widows and disabled, and there were many charitable organizations that saw to the basic needs of others. The Helping Hand Institute and Provident Association and other private agencies came to the rescue of thousands of unemployed in Kansas City during the autumn of 1909. A municipal department of public welfare was created in Kansas City on April 4, 1910. The public agency, however, was supported by voluntary private funds, not by taxes.

Soon politicians like Thomas J. Pendergast recognized the potential of government welfare as an instrument of political power. Before long, charity or welfare became a government function, but political charity is not charity at all. Government welfare spread rapidly to other cities, states, and then to the federal government. ". . . there is much evidence that the New Deal spending was designed with one overriding objective: to use money to buy votes to assure FDR's re-election (*How Capitalism Saved America*, 200)."

R. J. Rushdoony reported in his book, *The Nature of the American System:*

> The tremendous potentialities for political power were widely recognized. <u>Not charity but power</u> is the primary function of statist welfare. The attempts of various agencies in recent years to move faster than the public demand, and then to create by propaganda that public

demand, is motivated by a lust for power, not by a regard for human welfare. Charity is a by-product: there must be enough, like bread and circuses, to keep the masses happy, but the foremost goal is power, power to be gods and to manipulate men and society, in indulge the whims of megalomania in the name of benevolence. (22)

Should everyone have the right to vote? In the founding of this country it was the property owners that voted. Should those who pay no taxes decide how the money of those who financially support government is to be spent?

Benjamin Franklin, one of our Founding Fathers, is reported to have said, "When the people find they can vote themselves money that will herald the end of the republic."

When I was working as a financial planner, I sometimes worked with a CPA. We sat in his office one day in Memphis, Tennessee, and talked about all of the local, state, and federal taxes that we were paying. Just off the top of our heads we were able to identify fifty different taxes.

There are basically three kinds of taxes: <u>direct taxes</u>, <u>indirect taxes</u>, and <u>hidden taxes</u>.

> For example, one may pay a sales tax when he purchases a new radio. The purchaser is aware of paying that tax, but he is not aware of paying many other taxes that are included in the selling price. For instance, taxes have been paid on the labor that was required to produce the radio on raw materials that were needed in manufacturing the radio. Taxes have been paid on the

factory where the radio was manufactured. Transportation costs have been included in the selling price. The transportation companies that handled the radio have included a certain amount of taxes in their charges. Many of these taxes cannot be traced definitely to their original sources, but it has been estimated that hidden taxes represent almost twenty percent of every dollar of retail sales. (*Consumer Economics*, 238)

Let us suppose that we go into a retail store in Memphis and buy an item for $100.00. The hidden taxes included in the price is $20.00. But then 9% sales tax is added to the sales price so then we are paying $109.00 total for an item that would cost only $80.00 minus all taxes. This means that we are paying 36% tax on the item we purchase– with after tax dollars!

Taxpayer's Lament
Author unknown

Tax his land, tax his wage,
Tax his bed in he lays.
Tax his tractor, tax his mule,
Teach him taxes are the rule.

Tax his cow, tax his goat,
Tax his pants, tax his coat.
Tax his ties, tax his shirts,
Tax his work, tax his dirt.

Tax his tobacco, tax his drink,
Tax him if he tries to think.
Tax his booze, tax his beers,
If he cries, tax his tears.

Tax his bills, tax his gas,
Tax his notes, tax his cash.

Tax him good and let him know
That after taxes, he has no dough.

If he hollers, tax him more,
Tax him until he's good and sore.
Tax his coffin, tax his grave,
Tax the sod in which he lays.

Put these words upon his tomb,
"Taxes drove me to my doom!"
And when he's gone, we won't relax,
We'll still be after the inheritance TAX,
Hey maybe you'll get a refund!!

Accounts Receivable Tax
Building Permit Tax
CDL license Tax
Cigarette Tax
Corporate Income Tax
Dog License Tax
Federal Income Tax
Federal Unemployment Tax (FUTA)
Fishing License Tax
Food License Tax
Fuel permit tax Gasoline Tax (42 cents per gallon)
Hunting License Tax
Inheritance Tax Interest expense (tax on the B money)
Inventory Tax
IRS Interest Charges (tax on top of tax)
IRS Penalties (tax on top of tax)
Liquor Tax
Luxury Tax
Marriage License Tax
Medicare Tax
Property Tax
Real Estate Tax

Service charge Tax
Social Security Tax

Road usage Tax (Truckers)
Sales Tax
Recreational Vehicle Tax
School Tax
State Income Tax
State Unemployment Tax (SUTA)
Telephone federal excise Tax
Telephone federal universal service fee Tax
Telephone federal, state and local surcharge Tax
Telephone minimum usage surcharge Tax
Telephone recurring and non-recurring charges Tax
Telephone state and local Tax
Telephone usage charge Tax
Utility Tax
Vehicle License Registration Tax
Vehicle Sales Tax
Watercraft registration Tax
Well Permit Tax
Workers Compensation Tax

COMMENTS: Not one of these taxes existed 100 years ago and our
nation was the most prosperous in the world, had absolutely no national
debt, had the largest middle class in the world and Mom stayed home to raise
the kids.

What Happened?

We know that some taxes are necessary for the government to provide the service we truly need. However, many of the departments of our federal government are unnecessary and some are unconstitutional. Two books by Martin L. Gross expose the outlandish salaries and perks of our federal employees and politicians. The Pork Barrel spending is absolutely obscene. From the books, *The Government Racket* and *A Call for Revolution*, I hit just a few items of wasteful spending we taxpayers support:

$107.000 to study the sex life of the Japanese quail
$11 million for a private pleasure boat harbor in Cleveland
$150,000 to study the Hatfield-McCoy feud
$84,000 to find out why people fall in love
$1 million to study why people don't ride bikes to work
$144,000 to see if pigeons follow economic laws
$2 million to construct an ancient Hawaiian canoe
$160 to see if you can hex an opponent by drawing an "X" on his chest
$57,000 spent by the Executive Branch for gold-embossed playing cards.
$7 million to study air pollution in Mexico City
$1 million for a Utah study on how to cross the street safely
$100,000 to find out why people don't like beets
$90,000 to study the social life of vegetarians
$46,000 to find out how long it takes to cook eggs
$37,000 to study the handling of animal manure
$1 million to study brown tree snakes
$200,000 to celebrate Smokey the Bear's fiftieth anniversary

The Ten Commandments that were given by God to Moses were not for the Jews only but are incumbent on all men in every age. The eighth commandment establishes property rights, **"Thou shalt not steal."** Exodus 20:15. Arthur W. Pink states in his book, *The Ten Commandments,* "The positive duty here enjoined is: thou shalt by all proper means preserve and further both thine own and thy neighbor's estate (49)."

Charles Hodge remarks in Vol. III of *Systematic Theology*:

> This commandment forbids all violations of the rights of property. The right of property is an object in the right to its exclusive possession and use. The doctrine of the divine right of property is the only security for the individual or for society. (421) . . . As to the community of goods, it entered into the scheme of Plato's *Republic*, for in his view private property was the chief source of all social evils. Modern communism, on the contrary, so far as its general character is concerned, is materialistic and atheistic, and in some of its forms pantheistic. (430) It is a historical fact that communism had its origin in its modern form in materialistic atheism; (433) "Thou shalt not steal" forbids all unfair acquisition of the property of our neighbor. (436)

In the book, *The Ten Commandments* by G. Campbell Morgan, the following comments are made on the Eighth Commandment:

> The command is, in the first instance, a recognition of the rights of property. Man, in his relation to God, is ever compelled to own that nothing he possesses can be held to be outside of the right of divine interference. Man in relation to man can claim to possess, outside the

right of human interference, this being clearly recognized by the command. (90) Broadly stated, the eighth commandment forbids all forms of communism that deny man's right to property. (92)

Thomas Watson presents this exegesis on the eighth commandment in his book on the Ten Commandments:

> "Thou shalt not steal," the thing forbidden in this commandment is meddling with another man's property. The civil lawyers define *furtum,* stealth or theft to be, "the laying hands unjustly on that is another's; the invading of another's right. (164) For confutation of the doctrine of community, that all things are common, and one man has a right to another's estate, this is confuted by Scripture. When thou comest into the standing corn of thy neighbor, thou shalt not move a sickle unto thy neighbor's corn. Deut. 23:25. Property must be respected; God has set this eighth commandment as a hedge about a man's estate and this hedge cannot be broken without sin. (167)

During the Civil Rights movement some were using a slogan, "Human Rights are more important than Property Rights." What a puerile statement! Property rights *are* Human rights.

To confiscate someone's wealth or property in order to redistribute it is a sin whether done by an individual or a government. It is theft! Therefore communism and socialism is against the law of God.

Does the government or anyone else have the right to tell a business owner who he must hire and who can be fired? Is this not meddling with someone's property and is this not forbidden in the law of God?

T. Robert Ingram, in the *World Under God's Law* gives his opinion of an oppressive government:

> A man is accountable to the government for how he uses whatever he thinks he owns, but at any moment the government may rob him of it. The income tax, seizes property under the pain of the most severe punishment, virtually abolishes any man's control over what is his own, and substitutes full government regulation over all life for just punishment of crime. The state, is supposed to punish thieves, becomes itself a monster thief (97) . . . the law takes property from one person and gives it to another; the law takes the wealth of all and gives it to a few. (99)

Our government is obligated to protect us and punish the thieves and is the biggest thief of all. The U. S. Congress and the Obama administration in their socialistic agenda is truly the public enemy.

Many people associate covetousness with the rich, but it can also be found in those of meager means as this story of Mark Twain illustrates. Mark Twain was talking with a friend one day about a very successful man whom they both knew who had become quite rich. Mark Twain's friend remarked, "Yes, he has a lot of wealth, but it is tainted." To this Mark Twain replied, "Yes, but the worst thing is that it is twice tainted, for it taint yours and it taint mine!"

SOCIALISM AND EDUCATION

The duty and responsibility to educate our children was assigned by God to the parent. *"The fear of the Lord is the beginning of knowledge: but fools despise wisdom and instruction. My son, hear the instruction of thy father, and forsake not the law of thy mother."* Proverbs 117:8

"And ye shall teach then your children, speaking of them when thou sittest in thine house, and when thou walkest by the way, when thou liest down, and when thou risest up." Deuteronomy 11:19 In other words, in all conditions and on all occasions they were to be engaged in teaching, in giving instructions to their children. Education is still under parental control even when children are taught by tutors and schools. *"Now I say, that the heir, as long as he is a child, differeth nothing from a servant, though he is lord of all; but is under tutors and governors until the time appointed of the father."* Galatians 4:12

Robert E. Lee received his earliest education from his mother at home in his early years. Thomas Jefferson was home-educated. Jefferson founded the University of Virginia. He believed that tax subsidized elementary schools should be wholly governed by parents of the local neighborhoods who had children attending as students, not by any "general authority of the government" at a municipal, state, or federal level. In Jefferson's view, schools were to be a resource to be made available on a wholly voluntary basis. Compulsory education, compulsory attendance, legal coercion, and abrogation of parental custody or control of a child were utterly unacceptable to Jefferson. Any attempt to standardize education or obtain a uniformity of worldview in the population was also viewed to be inappropriate.

When the government system took over the schools and passed compulsive attendance laws, they were saying in essence, "Your children do not belong to you, they belong to us."

Horace Mann (1796-1858) aptly called the "Father of the Common Schools," was a Unitarian who attended the church of transcendentalist Theodore Parker. Parker was a radical abolitionist and one of the "secret six" who financed John Brown in his attempt to instigate a Haitian type uprising in the American South. Mann's closest associates were abolitionists. Mann believed that he would create a Utopia with his system of government schools. Mann shared with Robert Owen, the "father of Socialism," the erroneous creed that one is the product of one's intellectual ambiance and material surroundings. His Unitarian mind adhered to these major false theories:

1. <u>The child belongs to the State</u>, not the parents. He perhaps was so influenced by Plato's *Republic*.
2. <u>The clean slate theory</u> held by John Locke and others. This is a belief that every child comes into the world with a blank mind. This denies inherited characteristics, genes, DNA, or inherent intelligence. Horace Mann's theory also disregards the teaching in Matthew 25 where the Lord gives to his servants a different number of talents. Of course, a Unitarian has no regard for the Bible. The word, "educate," derived from the Latin, *"e"*- out *"duco"*- lead; means to bring out abilities and talents in the person and then to develop him in terms of himself (R. J. Rushdoony, *Intellectual Schizophrenia,* 7)
How can you help to bring out and develop inward talents and abilities if the child is a blank slate?" Mann's idea was not to educate but to indoctrinate and brainwash each child in the same values and beliefs. If the students had any preconceptions, they must be weaned from the past, home, nation, and religion. It was,

therefore, important to get the child away from the parental influence at the earliest possible age. Mann's agenda was basic to all Utopian thinking such as the Marxists.

3. <u>The Perfectibility of Man</u>. In the fifth century, the Doctrine of Original Sin and the Doctrines of Grace taught by St. Augustine was challenged. "Pelagius denied that human nature had been corrupted by sin. He maintained that the only ill effects the race had suffered as the result of Adam's transgression was the bad example he had set for mankind."[38] Augustine taught that men could never be entirely free from sin in this present life. "The two radical principles of Pelagianism are, first, that the nature of man is uninjured by the fall, so that men are free from sin until by voluntary transgression they incur guilt. Secondly, that our natural powers, since, as well as before the fall, are fully competent to render complete obedience to the law. From these principles Pelagius inferred, (1) that a man, even the heathen, might live from birth to death free from all sin, although he did not assert that any man ever had so lived. (2) That when converted, men might, and numbers of men did, live without sin; perfectly obeying the law. (3) That this obedience was rendered in the exercise of their ability, assisted by the Grace of God."[39] Not only was the Pelagian Theory contrary to the Holy Scriptures but it could not be demonstrated that any human being of any race or at any time did ever live without sin. Pelagians were condemned in the Council of Carthage, A. D. 418.

4. The Arminian system as held by the Wesleyans and advocated by the Oberlin University in Ohio believed in the possibility of entire or full sanctification in this present life. They believed that a Christian can be so

---

[38] David Steele and Curtis Thomas, *The Five Points of Calvinism*, Philadelphia: Presbyterian and Reformed Publishing Company, 20.
[39] Charles Hodge, *Systematic Theology, Vol. VIII*, Grand Rapids: William B. Eerdmans Publishing, 250.

filled by the Holy Spirit so as to live above sin in sinless perfection in the present life. This is sometimes referred to as full sanctification or as "getting the Holy Ghost." God does intend to complete the salvation and sanctification of His people when these vile bodies are changed at the end of our earthly lives.

Although each Christian is exhorted to pursue holiness it is never attained in this present life according to the testimony of Holy Scriptures. The wise man said, *"These is not a just man upon earth, that doeth good, and sinneth not." Eccles. 7:20* At a later period of his life, St. Paul said, *"Not as though I had already attained, either were already perfect: but I follow after, if that I may apprehend that for also I am apprehended of Christ Jesus, Brethren, I count not myself to have apprehended: but this one thing I do, forgetting those things are behind and reaching forth unto these things are before, I press toward the mark for the prize of the high calling of God in Christ Jesus." Philippians 3: 12-14*

James the Just declared in James 3:2, *"In many things, we offend all."*

The disciple whom Jesus loved proclaimed, *"If we say that we have no sin, we deceive ourselves, and the truth is not in us." 1 John 1:8*

Horace Mann probably never knew of the proposition of perfectibility set forth by Pelagius or Wesley but being a secular humanist, he believed in perfectibility through social action.

R. J. Rushdooney sums up the belief of Horace Mann in his book, *This Independent Republic* in this manner:

This is what Mann believed:

> . . .evil is not in human nature, is either good or at least neutral, but is in the environment. Man is hence malleable. The state, by reordering the environment, will be able to create a perfect humanity. "By changing human institutions human nature itself will be born again. Redemption is thus political action, not religious faith, and statism is made necessary to man.
> Horace Mann in education held that state schools would eliminate crime, slums, prisons, and all human ills; socialists held that state actions will accomplish the same purpose through politico-economic legislation; the champions of a welfare economy or interventionism believe that housing projects will end slums, poverty and delinquency. (138)

Richard T. LaPiere (1899 –1986) was a professor (Emeritus) of sociology at Stanford University from 1929 to 1965. He called attention to how advocates of public schools have maintained that they, ". . . would, in a generation or two, be the cure for every recognized social ill; and that the schools would, moreover, in the course of time, cost the tax-payer nothing, since the educated boys would grow up to be reasonable and honest men and the need for public support of jails, prisons, poor farms, and homes for the aged indigent would thus be eliminated." Dr. Russell Kirk, American traditional conservative, noted that the public schools did not accomplish these Utopian expectations, education was made compulsory and expanded to girls. Finally, Professor Frederick Eby of the University of Texas wrote, "One conclusion is certain: the strong claims of [over] a century ago that a system of public schools would do away with crime now look absurd. . . . Not only has public education failed to eliminate crime but it is in some measure responsible for the increase of these various evils. . . .[40]

Will a change of environment bring perfection as Horace Mann and many others have believed?

> As Paul Harvey put it, "You never heard of Jesus worrying about moving people out of the slums. He walked the squalid streets from end to end . . . getting the slums out of the people. Until that is done, moving the people merely moves the slums. Witness the appalling conditions in many of the new government-financed housing projects, some of have become so crime and filth-ridden as to become uninhabitable. There they stand, battered ruins, too dangerous to for human beings to live in. (Kershner, 36)

A change of environment has no transforming power. You can take a hog out of the hog-pen, bathe him, perfume him, and tie a pretty bow around his neck. Turn him loose in your living room. What will happen? The hog will not change, but your living room will. Education has no transforming power as to moral behavior. Educate a thief and you will have a smarter thief. Educate a fool and you will have a sillier fool. True change of character and reformation can only be effective by the Divine Grace of God. Recently I heard an educator, who alleges that he is a conservative, when trying to raise more money to build new schools say, "We can build more jails or we can build more schools." The radical spirit of Robert Owen, Horace Mann, and their partisans still lives today.

---

[40] T. Robert Ingram, *Schools Weighed in the Balance*, Houston, Texas: St. Thomas Press, 15.

John Dewey (1859-1952) continued on Horace Mann's path to socialism with a new vigor. He has been called the "father of progressive education," the "father of modern education," and also the "father of the experiential education movement." Like Mann, he believed that state education was the answer to bring about the socialist state. This meant that teachers must indoctrinate pupils into the socialized order. John Dewey identified himself as a "democratic socialist."

> Dewey had a strong faith in change, change at least until the Great Community was born. His principle of approval was change, change, however understood only as rebellion against religion, capitalism and individualism. Any return to such things was not change but retrogression.[41]

I wonder if Dewey ever called this "change we can believe in?" Dewey wanted a classless society that would outlaw both failure and success in order to equalize man. He was a singer of the Humanist manifesto, which is akin to the communist manifesto.

During World War II my family moved to Detroit, Michigan. There I received my first taste of Marxism taught in the public schools. As a student in the fourth grade, I was taught the glorious virtues of communist Russia. I remember to this day the tune and some of the words of a Soviet patriotic song we were required to learn and sing in school:

"Onward, ride onward, men onward,
Over our own homeland . . .

---

[41] Rousas J. Rushdooney, *The Messianic Character of American Education*, Nutley, New Jersey: The Craig Press, 148.

Ride past the factories, fields, and farms,
Belonging to us one and all together . . .

HUMANISM UNMASKED

As Defined By John Dewey, THE FATHER OF MODERN EDUCATION

Humanism is as old as the garden of Eden, but few know what it is. The idea of Humanism replacing Godism can be seen in the garden of Eden when Satan taught Eve that she would no longer need God, she could be as her own god and do what she pleased after she got enough knowledge of her own.

The Humanist Manifesto reveals a large picture of intent shaped for education by Dewey. It also shows a picture of what our government is doing, since it has been modified greatly by graduates of this modern system of education.

Please note the U.S. Dept. of Education did not exist until Lyndon B. Johnson as President. Such a department was never intended by the Founding Fathers. They didn't even want their children fed by the government, much less taught what to think by the ruling powers.

John Dewey had great influence in the National Education Association and reshaping America's schools. He has had a profound influence on generations of educators. John Dewey, the Father of Modern American Education, wrote *The Human*ist *Manifesto* in 1933.

After reading and correspondence with Europe, John Dewey, *the father of modern education*, traveled to Europe, China, and Turkey in the early nineteen thirties.

Upon his return to America, he helped author and did sign the Humanist Manifesto was the Americanized version of the *Communist Manifesto* penned by Karl Marx.

The Humanist Manifesto was signed by many prominent people. Since then a second, called The Humanist Manifesto II has been written and signed by many more. The list of individuals, corporations, and trust funds is impressive with its power to influence. We come to see that the National Humanist Foundation, Society for the Humanities, and other such names do have a common philosophy and intent.

Seeing how great is the list of those who have publicly and openly endorse humanism in one way or another, it becomes clear that a common system of thought drives many sources of great economic and political power.

That document, Humanist Manifesto and its follow up, Humanist Manifesto II, define a collectively held goal of many political-economic powers.

Philosophers have written on the subject since Plato and Aristotle. Later writers include French revolutionaries such as Rousseau in throwing off the authority of kings, and then Engels and Karl Marx. . . .

Growth of the concept was slow for the first few thousand years of recorded history, until French and European philosophers further developed some of the details prior to the French Revolution. Then in 1859, Darwinism gave accelerated growth through the concepts of evolution, relativism and positivism.

Law courses adopted the ideas of "relativism" and "positivism" in major universities as early as 1870.

By 1940, **relative law** or case law also called evolutionary law had replaced the absolute standard of **original intent law**. . . Other authors have books with the same title showing how different the new law interprets our Constitution by the changed standards of relativism.

A 1996 book, *Original Intent*, published by Wallbuilders with a four way index contrasting the original intent of our Constitution and how it has been changed, should be in all our schools. This contrast is clearly shown by original documents from those great men who signed the Declaration of Independence and the U.S. Constitution and other documents of that time.

Relativism as a positive gain relative to man's changing standards became popularized by the educational elite. Educators said since man evolves, his society evolves, and therefore his law must also change to fit the changing man. That's how the evolution of Charles Darwin impacted law, society, government, politics, economics of teaching in text book sales, as well as science in all its branches. Not only biology would change from Creationism to Evolution, but physics and math would change from Ordered Systems to Chaos as a focus of teaching.

Oliver Wendell Holmes, Jr. (1841-1935) served as an associate justice on the Supreme Court from 1902 to 1932. He was the first graduate of "relative" legal standards interpretation. His greatest influence on the Supreme Court began around 1920. By 1940 the absolute standards of *Blackstone's Law Commentary* had been discarded nearly everywhere. Blackstone had been the standard of law interpretation since the British courts were developed. Blackstone based all understanding on God, and natural law that came forth from God, and man's government law as derived from nature that was created by God. He believed in God, an absolute God, and he accepted an absolute system of law that like God did not change.

Positivism says that what is a perceived gain, a plus, is a good thing. The plus or minus is measured from the relative point of view of an individual, not any absolute standard. Positivism along with Relativism are the basis of saying "The end justifies the means."

Humanism with its relative and subjective values feeds systems like, I'm OK. You're OK. Tolerance in a big way. No absolutes. Each person establishes his own system of values as he sees fit with no absolutes or external authorities.

This results in calling them bigots who would impose any external authority or absolute standard of reference to right and wrong. It allows for saying the end justifies whatever means it takes to get a gain. So long as that gain seems to me as being a positive gain relative to how I see things, that's what I call good.

Humanism says forget the absolutes. Judge things by what seems to be right for you, just like Satan tempted Eve in the garden.

The core idea being that Humanism as a system denies God, and Jesus as the Son of God who said that only God is Good.

Removal of God from the value system was done not only in the Bolshevik revolution but also in the Humanist Manifesto. Having no absolute standard leaves then only each individual to define his own ideas of what "feels good" to him.

Humanism has existed from the beginning of time. It was defined in the garden of Eden where Satan used his most tempting bait to cause Eve first to doubt and then to ignore the word of God. "...you shall be as gods...".

Humanism cannot be seen in its biggest context from its own point of view. Humanism denies God so it denies the total context. Only in a faith towards God can Humanism be seen for what it is in the highest context.

To those who believe in God, Humanism is man's way of saying, exactly what the Humanists proclaim, man must be his own god. That means to a Christian, rebellion against God.

The first rebellion was in the garden of Eden. It was over the idea of being as a god, self-directing and without further need of Almighty God. Thus the oldest Biblical word for what we call Humanism is rebellion against God Almighty.

Most literature on humanism does not speak of rebellion against God. However humanistic writings were used to inspire rebellions against government in many places. Most notably, the Bolshevik Revolution clearly and openly denounced God.

Humanism has been manifest since Eve was tempted to do away with her need for Almighty God and be her own god through partaking of all knowledge.

Humanism is nothing but a redefined label for the rebellion against God that happened in the garden, by adding to and taking from the truth of his word so to justify mankind in doing its own thing, whatever that may be.

The hearts of our children are the goal of those who have taught against absolutes and encouraged "relative positivism" as a way of thinking based on loose association and calling it higher order thinking.

Be on guard. Be not deceived when you see those fine sounding phrases of "Changes in education for excellence" or "higher order thinking" or "critical thinking"; because most of those actions covered by those words are used to destroy faith in God.

Viewpoint from the "New History:" Consider this viewpoint from the *New Standard of American History*:

> "Man emerged from the slime of a soupy organic ocean as he evolved from a protozoa cell to higher and higher forms."

So man is growing up. There was not a fall as the Bible teaches, but an upward evolution and therefore no need for a Savior. And as the humanists write, *if man is going to be saved, he must do it himself.* . . .

Excerpts from "The World's Oldest False Religion," (http://www.christianparents.com/humanism.htm)

Humanist Manifesto I and II, Encyclopedia Britannica,
1952, Vol. 7, 297.

John Dewey was born in 1859, the year of Darwin's publication of *Origin of the Species*. The theory of evolution gave impetus to Dewey's belief in the perfectibility of man. Since man had advanced so far from lower species, how much higher could he go! The Godless theory of evolution at one time tells us that man is little better than an ape, and at another time that he is little less than a god. Today, the philosophical theory of evolution, is being taught in most public (government or state) schools today as a scientific fact either directly or indirectly. When children are taught in our schools that man is nothing more than a clever animal it is not surprising when they begin to act like animals.

Those who believe in cosmic evolution and say that this world came into being by a great cosmic accident deny the God of creation. To believe that this universe is the result of a cosmic accident is not even logical! All laws, whether in the field of chemistry or physics are simply derived from human experience and human observation. The law of gravity is simply a generalization based on human experience that when we release a heavier-than-air object in a normal atmospheric environment, then the object will fall toward the center of the earth. Other laws are likewise predicated on human observation.

There is no evidence to support the derivation of a law that accidents produce synchronizing systems. Accidents may produce substances like rubber, but never in the course of human history has an accident, volcanic eruption, earthquake, produced a vacuum cleaner, a sewing machine, a watch, or a computer. Every synchronizing system or machine has always had a creator behind it! This world and universe is such a synchronizing system that a watch company can get its time from the stars.

The theory of organic evolution is disproved by the second law of thermodynamics. This law of physics states that heat gradually escapes, things go from order to disorder and all things have a tendency to decay and age. If you don't believe this, just do look at yourself in the mirror.

No evidence of evolution can be observed today. Bulls and cows still reproduce "after their kind." Cows do not give birth to goats. There is no evidence of evolution occurring at present; furthermore there is no evidence that evolution has transpired in the past.

Since transmutation or the evolutionary process cannot be observed as taking place in the present time the evolutionist tells us that the process is *too slow to be observed*. Therefore they need billions of years to support this theory. Scientists have developed dating systems to back up their claims. All of these dating systems are based on a supposition that change has always occurred at a constant rate. This, of course, can never be validated because it was never observed by man and recorded. Even if the earth is very old it would be no problem to the creationist because God could have created the earth with age. Adam was created with age. He came into being not as a baby but as a full grown and mature man.

Some time ago I attended a conference on education hosted by (the late) T. Robert Ingram, headmaster of St. Thomas Episcopal School, Houston, Texas. One of the speakers was Dr. Harold Slusher of the University of Texas, El Paso. He spoke on the different dating systems used by scientists and explained how they were all unreliable. The University of Texas had tested and recorded the rate of decay or weakening of the earth's magnetic field. Calculating that the present rate of decay had always been consistent, their researchers proved that the magnetic field would have been so strong ten thousand years ago as to make life on earth impossible. Of course, this system, like all dating systems, was based on presupposition. But if the rate of decay has always been absolute we have a very young earth. Dr. Slusher spoke of other dating methods that pointed to the earth as being comparatively young.

Dr. Werner von Braun (1912-1977) was one of the greatest scientists of the twentieth century. When Germany collapsed at the end of WWII, he and his team surrendered to the Americans. The reason given was that Werner von Braun wanted to work for a people who were guided by the Bible. Von Braun, a life-long Lutheran, was a believer in intelligent design in the universe long before it became a catch phrase and a lightning rod of debate.

> For me, the idea of a creation is not conceivable without invoking the necessity of design. One cannot be exposed to law and order of the universe without concluding there must be design and purpose. . . . They challenge science to prove the existence of God. But must one really light a candle to see the sun? The incomprehensible size of the universe is woven of immeasurable power. Yet it is arranged on meticulous precision to support life in Earth. Truly these facts form a shining beam from the Creator that dwarfs the sun itself!

The ability of Earth to sustain intelligent life in turn was capable of creating machines designed to explore the moon and the planets was clear evidence to von Braun that man and his universe were the creation of God. His gravestone reads:

Werner Von Braun

1912-1977

> "The heavens are telling the glory of God and the firmament proclaims his handiwork." Psalms 19:1

Although the "theory of evolution" is taught in most "public" schools today, it was not always so. The socialistic agenda of Mann and Dewey has been slowed down greatly because of the individualistic American spirit and the Christians and conservatives within the school system. However, in the majority of the schools today, the Bible and prayer are now forbidden. History books have been changed drastically to promote a socialistic agenda. The public schools are worse today than they were yesterday and they are better today than they will be tomorrow.

Those who home school or send their children to private or parochial schools must still pay taxes to support state schools. Every citizen needs to be concerned about what goes on in state education and halt to the best of our ability the social and anti-Christian agenda. We have often heard the cry, "We must save our public schools!" To this I reply, "No, we must save our children."

It is intentional that our general public should be so defensive of "our public schools." For many years they have been so conditioned and programmed. The National Citizens Commission for Public Schools was incorporated in May 1949 to offset unfriendly criticism of the so-called "enemies" of public schools. One of their early officers, Robert A. Skaife let slip the real agenda of this organization way back in its early days. "Resistance to such pressures is automatic when the schools and the community thought of as inseparable."[42] The attack on the schools is then

---

[42] T. Robert Ingram, *Schools Weighed in the Balance*, 3.

considered, as it should be an attack on the community." Thus, criticism of public schools is synonymous with treason!

Actually there are no "public" schools that I know of today. A public school existed many years ago when the parents of a newly settled frontier town would come together to build a school house and subsequently engage a teacher to teach their children. Attendance was voluntary. These days what are commonly called public schools are in reality state or government schools. We now have a federal Department of Education that is unconstitutional according to Article 1, section 8 of the constitution. It came into being under Lyndon B. Johnson. This federal agency wastes billions of the tax payers' dollars and does not teach a single student. The lunacy of federal involvement in education can be seen in George W. Bush's dim-witted and deceptive "No Child Left Behind" Act. This act has been soundly denounced by George Will, Walter Williams, and Pat Buchanan as "teaching to the test."

Excerpts from "The Trouble with No Child Left Behind"

Internet Blog von Mises Daily: Tuesday, March 23, 2010 by Anton Batey

On January 8th, 2002, President Bush signed into law the No Child Left Behind Act (NCLB), intended to improve proficiency in math and reading. It sets the expectation of 100% compliance among Title One public schools by 2013 or 2014. It passed in the House on 13 May 2001 by 384–45, and it passed in the Senate on 14 June 2001 by 91–8.

According to the bill, students in the schools must pass standardized tests. If an insufficient number pass the first year, there are no sanctions.[1] If the school's students fail a second year, then "technical assistance" is provided, whereby parents can send their children to different schools. If the parents decide to do so, then the transportation is provided by the school district of where the child lives. If the school fails a third year, then the school must pay for supplemental educational services for the students. If they fail a fourth year, then management restructuring takes place. On the fifth year of failure, all staff are replaced, and the school could turn into a charter or private school.

There are rare instances where extreme advocates on both the Left and Right agree on public policy and are opposed to a specific program. This is one of those instances, and for good reason. Notable and respected conservative George Will claims that the program "spawned lowered standards."[5] Walter E. Williams, another respected conservative and a professor of economics at George Mason University, condemned the program "that billions of dollars are spent on." He argues that "without a civilized learning environment, academic excellence is impossible no matter how much money is spent."[6] Former Republican presidential nominee Pat Buchanan denounced the program as part of Bush's "big government," rhetorically asking "what Republican ran last time for cutting back George Bush's big government?... Who stood up and said no to No Child Left Behind?"[7]

Noted economist Milton Friedman said, shortly before his death, regarding the program, "Recent federal legislation in the No Child Left Behind Act requires all states to develop regular performance measures of student learning and to make these measures publicly available. As for the typical parent who still believes his or her child attends an above-average school, what will happen when many of them learn they are wrong?" Libertarian Charles Murray said that the program "set a goal that was devoid of any contact with reality."[8]

Of course, many left-liberals are opposed to the program as well. Al Franken, for instance, in his book *Lies and the Lying Liars Who Tell Them* criticized the NCLB program, saying that since "Congress authorized a $5.6 billion increase in Title One spending for low income children," and "President Bush budgeted only $1 billion for Title One ... if Title One calls for $2,800 per poverty-level student," then "1,643,857" children will be "left behind" (pp. 349–351). Prominent socialist James Flynn, in his debate with Charles Murray in 2006, also criticized the Act.

Barack Obama said of the act, "don't come up with this law called *No Child Left Behind* and then leave the money behind.... Don't tell us that you'll put high-quality teachers in every classroom and then leave the support and the pay for those teachers behind.... Don't label a school as failing one day and then throw your hands up and walk away from it the next."

The No Child Left Behind legislation has vastly increased standardized tests and created a muddle of federal regulations with results opposite from their intentions.

At first glance, the concept of standardized tests seems reasonable. Children should be tested, and the tests are clear indicators either of how intelligent they are or of how much the school is teaching them. But what is the school "teaching" them, exactly? The answer is simple but unfortunate: they're teaching them how to *take the test*.

Linda Valli, Maryland associate professor of education, conducted a long study on the federal program and determined that standardized testing "actually undermined the quality of teaching in reading and math" and that the decline in teacher quality and tangible information being taught to the students is because of "the pressure teachers were feeling to 'teach to the test.'"

Alfie Kohn, author of over a dozen books on education, parenting, and anthropology, decries NCLB's "overemphasis on standardized testing and punitive sanctions." He generally disparages the program, saying that the "law is not about narrowing the achievement gap; its main effect has been to sentence poor children to an endless regimen of test-preparation drills." And furthermore, "even if the scores do rise, it's at the expense of a quality education."[9] According to a 50-state survey by Teachers Network, a nonprofit education organization, only 3% of teachers think No Child Left Behind helps them teach more efficiently.

NCLB is simply a way for the federal government to tighten its grip on schools by threatening them with punishment. Those who control the schools control the future. The tests and regulations indirectly control what children learn in school (and what they do not learn in school).

"Those who control the schools control the future."

More importantly, what are the results of the program? One should keep in mind, however, what Kohn said regarding the scores: the higher test scores may come at the cost of learning. However, in 2006, for example, math and reading test scores dropped significantly, showing that only 32% of high-school students were proficient in math.[10]

What about high-school graduation rates? Surely the rate of graduations is reflective of school quality and efficiency, No Child Left Behind was supposed to improve. In 2008, a report sponsored by America's Promise Alliance, was prepared by the Editorial Projects in Education Research Center, showed that schools in major cities in the United States had a horrible 52% graduation rate after four years; the national average is 70%, still isn't good. In areas like Baltimore, with a graduation rate of 34%, Columbus, with a graduation rate of 41%, and Detroit, with an awful rate of 25%, their suburbs are at 80% or higher.[11] These urban areas were supposed to be the ones No Child Left Behind would target.

Roughly 1.2 million students drop out every year, according to researchers.[12] Thus, any test-score improvement is itself only representative of those who are still in school.

Most important, perhaps, is the fact that the No Child Left Behind Act is completely unconstitutional. There's nothing in the Constitution that permits the federal government getting involved in education. This fact was ignored by President George W. Bush, who, in November 2005, infamously referred to the US Constitution as "just a [G. D.] piece of paper."[13] In February 2005, a bipartisan panel of state lawmakers concluded that the program is unconstitutional since it trumps state and local control over schools.[14] They claim that "This assertion of federal authority into an area historically reserved to the states has had the effect of curtailing additional state innovations and undermining many that had occurred during the past three decades."

Some claim that, since participation in NCLB is optional at the state level, it's not coercive at the federal level. This excuse is ridiculous, and the same federal/state policies apply with highway funds if BAC isn't lowered to .08, for instance. Opting out doesn't mean they don't get taxed (via their citizens) in proportion to the money not spent by the feds on education, so it's really not much of an option. Tax money is extracted out of the state, and then states are given the "option" to participate in the program in order to get some of that money back. It's passive-aggressive coercion. Optional or not, the federal government has no authority to be involved in education.

Many people who support the program applaud the vast sums of money that are sunk into it. Is money the answer? The author of *Savage Inequalities*, Jonathan Kozol, thinks so. According to him, "grossly insufficient funding" is to blame for poor results in Chicago. Kozol claims that the children's "problems stem from short funding," and that the "low funding of the schools that they attend confirm the wisdom" that more funding is necessary. Kozol does, however, concede that "it is obvious that urban schools have other problems in addition to their insufficient funding."

In 1984, a federal judge in Missouri ordered that the property tax in Kansas City be doubled, the income tax be increased, and other state funds be redirected in order to give Kansas City schools an extra $2 billion ($4.1 billion in 2008). In 1991, Kansas City was spending $9,412 per student, compared with $2,854 to $5,956 in the suburbs. Kansas City schools were furnished with brand new textbooks, state of the art computers, an Olympic-sized swimming pool, television studios, and even funding for *taxi* drivers to drive children to school if there were any problems with bus fare! According to those who believe money is the answer, this would be the place to see success. Did the test scores of students increase? Not even a little.[15]

In conclusion, it's apparent that government intervention in schools is an utter failure. The notions that standardized tests will fix the problem and that pouring money into a government project will churn out superior results are likewise absurd.

Why would anyone be opposed to this? Teaching to the test, increasing government centralization, and forcing teachers to turn into robots by mandating nearly everything they teach has been shown to be a failure.

Schools operate as a taxpayer-funded monopoly, answering unconstitutionally to the federal government and the teacher's union. Further, since it is a monopoly run by a coercive monopoly, it has all the attendant problems, i.e., it has no profit-loss mechanism. This monopoly is also subject to the whims of politicians, who can mandate that something either be taught or not taught as dictated by their beliefs. These beliefs are thus foisted upon the kids, who are required by law to study the given material *or else*.

Notes

[1] Technically, it's a little more complicated than that. The bureaucrats generally subdivide students into groups such as Blacks, Native Americans, Whites, Students with Special Needs, etc.
If just one of those groups fails to meet standards, the whole school will "fail." So a more accurate title for the program would be "No *Group* Left Behind."
[1] "LBJ Announces 88 New Projects," *Lodi News-Sentential*, 18 Jan. 1965.
[2] Chomsky, Noam. *Understanding Power*. The New Press, 2002.
[3] "Bush, GOP Senators Lick Wounds but Say They're Not Too Conservative", *Chicago Tribune*, 25 May 2001.
[4] "On Way to Passage, Bush's Education Plan Gets a Makeover", *The New York Times*, 4 May 2001.
[5] George Will, "Getting Past 'No Child,'" *The Washington Post*, 9 Dec. 2007.
[7] Buchanan, Pat, "Even in Massachusetts, Trouble for the Party of Government," *The Union Leader*, 19 Jan. 2010.
[8] Murray, Charles, "The Age of Educational Romanticism," *The New Criterion*, May 2008.
[9] Kohn, Alfie, "NCLB: 'Too Destructive to Salvage,'" *USA Today*, 31 May 2007.
[10] Walsh, James, "Math, Reading Test Scores Drop; Only 32% of High Schoolers Were Proficient in Math on Test Designed to Match Stiffer Learning Standard," *Star Tribune*, 15 Nov. 2006.
[11] Here are some other city/suburb splits:
New York — 47.4 percent vs. 82.9 percent
Cleveland — 42.2 percent vs. 78.1 percent
Philadelphia — 49.2 percent vs. 82.4 percent
Chicago — 55.7 percent vs. 84.1 percent
Los Angeles — 57.1 percent vs. 77.9 percent
Atlanta — 46.1 percent vs. 61.8 percent
[12] Grey, Berry, "High-School Drop Out Rate in Major US Cities at Nearly 50 Percent," *World Socialist*, 3 April 2008.
[13] Thompson, Doug, "Bush — Constitution 'Just a Goddamned Piece of Paper,'" *Op Ed News*, 11 Dec. 2005.
[14] Dillon, Sam, "Bipartisan Study Assails No Child Left Behind Act," *The New York Times*, 23 Feb. 2005
[15] "Desegregation's Broken Promises," *Forbes.com*, 10 Nov. 2003.
[16] Williams, Walter, "Dumbest Generation Getting Dumber," *Creators Syndicate Inc.*, 2009.[43]

In England many years ago, the churches felt the great need of educating not only the elite of society, but they wanted to reach the masses who could not afford to pay for education. Many of them strained themselves to the limit to provide education for as many of the masses of mankind as they possibly could. Most of the time the Sunday School and the day school were the same. Those that they had in their Sunday school were the pupils they would take during the week to teach history and the Three Rs. Theology was infused into all of their subjects. As the churches attempted to reach out more and more to the masses of men, they found that the financial burden was tremendous. The government of England realized that they were doing a great service for the country and began to give financial aid to the schools. They began to give more aid and with the financial aid came rules and regulations and gradually the private aspect of those schools faded away and education in England became government education.

---

[43] (http://mises.org/daily/4170)

A child prodigy who grew up to be short on practical judgment, English philosopher and social reformer, Jeremy Bentham (1748-1842) reasoned in accord with his utopian socialism, "If we can get universal and compulsory education, then by the end of the century all our political and moral problems will have been solved."

English artist, socialistic thinker, and eccentric loon John Ruskin, (1819-1900) bolstered the ideology that the "state" knows what is best for the children— not the parents. Like so many other socialists, he drew from Plato's *Republic* the recommendation that children should become common to all, i.e. the government's possession; hence, Ruskin's advised in 1867, "To effect [full care of children], the government must have authority over the people...."

In America there were no government schools until the year 1837. Up until that time all schools were private, most of them being church related from elementary, secondary, and even at the college level. In 1860, 90% of the education was private and Christian education. After Mr. Lincoln's War, the acceleration of statist education was significant.

Influenced by all of these promoters of "Progressive Education," and following them credulously, Hillary Clinton wrote *It Takes a Village* (1996) to persuade parents that they are incompetent to bring up their own flesh and blood. Accordingly the better-quality government should step in and shape the "tabula rasa" [blank slate] minds of their children so they will think the way the government wants them to think, thus making for a more harmonious, smooth-running machine of utopian socialism.

It has worked out as planned. Americans have finally turned out a generation trained to elect a socialist like Barack Obama. The masses have been "dumbed down" and are now easier for "Big Brother" or whomever to control.

Dr. Steve Wilson states in his book, *Bankruptcy of America*:

> The inability of America's education system to generate world class quality became increasingly evident during the eighties.
> America's school system seemed to provide the worst of all worlds; poor results *and* high costs. American educators had better ideas than their forebears. Not only was prayer out of the schools, but so too, it seemed, was anything that smacked of traditional American values. Courses seemed more geared toward exposing what was wrong with America and its ruling elites. Probably nowhere was there a better measure of the dismal failure of the new approach than in New York City. The city's public school system served 900,000 students at an average yearly cost of $6,700. In some New York high schools, as few as 25 percent of students graduated and the dropout rate averaged 30 percent city-wide. A study by the Rand Corporation found that only the top one-sixth of students took the Scholastic Aptitude Test (SAT) but, nevertheless, performed poorly: an average score of 632 out of a possible 1600.
> New York's 140 Catholic schools, many of which were located in the economically depressed areas of Harlem and the South Bronx, enrolled over 51,000 students, 85 percent of whom were black, Hispanic, or Asian. The Catholic schools had a one percent high school dropout rate, sent 90 percent of their graduates to college and spent just $1,900 per student. The same Rand study examined public school performance found that three-quarters of the Catholic school students took the SAT,

> and achieved an average score of 804. While New York's public schools employed 7,000 bureaucrats to administer their authoritarian version of academic freedom, the Catholic school system employed just 35 people in its central office.
>
> Despite their unquestionably superior performance, America's private schools were fighting a government-subsidized monopoly. (174-175)

At first the private schools wanted to be free of government control and be a real alternative to state schools. However, it was not long before many of these schools yielded to pressure and sought state accreditation and wanted teachers certified by the state. The government no longer sees the need to oppose private education as long as they control it. The cost of private education began to soar as many schools built costly new facilities. Mark Twain when asked to define a school replied, " A school is a teacher sitting on one end of a log with a student seated on the other end of the log." New expensive school buildings with high tech computers and science labs paid for by your tax dollars do not translate into a better quality education.

Archibald Alexander Hodge, Princeton theologian, saw the statist claim that "self-preservation" of the state required statist education and made these remarks:

> I am as sure as I am of Christ's reign that a comprehensive and centralized system of national education, separated from religion, as is now commonly proposed, will prove the most appalling enginery for the propagation of anti-Christian and atheistic unbelief and of anti-social nihilistic ethic, individual, social, and

political, this sin-rent world has ever seen. The tendency is to hold that this system must be altogether secular. The atheistic doctrine is gaining currency, even among professed Christians and even among some bewildered Christian ministers, that an education provided by the common government should be entirely emptied of all religious character. The Protestants object to the government schools being used for the purpose inculcating the doctrines of the Catholic Church, and Romanists object to the use of the Protestant version of the Bible and to the inculcation of the peculiar doctrines of the Protestant churches. The Jews protest against the schools being used to inculcate Christianity in any form, and the atheists and agnostics protest against any teaching that implies the existence and moral government of God. It is capable of exact demonstration that if every party in the state has the right of excluding from the public schools whatever he does not believe to be true, then he that believes most must give way to him that believes least, and then he that believes least must give way to him that believes absolutely nothing, no matter in how small a minority the atheists or the agnostics may be. It is self-evident that on this scheme, if it is consistently and persistently carried to in all parts of the country, the United States system of national popular education will be the most efficient and wide instrument for the propagation of Atheism the world has ever seen.[44]

One of the most astute observers of the causes and consequences of the changes in American society and of the growing influence of these utopian dreamers during the nineteenth century was a Presbyterian theologian, Robert Lewis Dabney.

---

[44] A. A. Hodge, *Popular Lectures on Theological Themes,* 280,283

Dabney was a close friend of General Thomas J. (Stonewall) Jackson, who served as Jackson's chief of staff during the early part of the Valley Campaign in Virginia. After the war, Dabney continued to preserve the truth about the history of the war and its long-tem effects upon American society in general. In January of 1879 Dabney publicly cautioned of the undesirable effects upon the moral character of America by the establishment of a "free" school system. Dabney warned that this action would eventually result in the removal of all Christian values and the Bible itself from the public school system. Dabney states, "We have again and again warned ". . . that the practical result . . . will enable the infidel party to triumph everywhere, to expel the Bible and Christianity from all schools, and to rear us (so far as state schools go) a generation of Atheists. This is to be the practical issue of their misguided zeal."

Dabney's prophecy has come to pass not only in public schools but also in community life in general. God has been removed from many modern public school systems, and nativity displays and even the exhibits of the Ten Commandments have been removed from public view. Dabney's 1879 prediction about the result of America embracing the values those utopian dreamers has become true. His predictions of the loss of proper moral values and the resulting sexual revolution resonate with uncanny accuracy. Dabney had a unyielding Biblical worldview in common with the founders of the United States. His competence in foreseeing various future problems in American society was because he understood the dissimilarities in worldviews of the communists, socialists, and secular humanists who held that man is capable of solving all his problems without any help from God and of building a near perfect world (Kennedy and Benson, 201).

In conclusion, consider this quote from Thomas Paine, one of the early supporters of the separation of this country from England. He is thought of as a Deist, and he most certainly went too far and became swept up in and carried away with the follies of the French Revolution. Today he has become the darling of the secular humanists who are always bleating, "Separation of church and state! Separation of church and state! Surely of all people he would approve of the secular government school system of today. The words of Thomas Paine, "Deist" condemn the government school system:

> In a speech he delivered in Paris on January 16, 1797, Thomas Paine harshly criticized what the French were then teaching in their science classes-especially the philosophy they were using. Interestingly, that same science philosophy of Thomas Paine was so critical is identical to that used in our public schools today. Paine's indictment of that philosophy is particularly significant in light of the fact that all historians today concede that Thomas Paine was one of the very least religious of our Founders. Yet, even Paine could not abide teaching science, excluded God's work and hand in the creation of the world and of all scientific phenomena. Below is an excerpt from that speech.
>
> (While Benjamin Franklin was serving in London as diplomat from the Colonies to the King, Franklin met Englishman Thomas Paine (born 1737, died 1809). Franklin arranged for him to move to America in 1774 and helped set him up in the printing business. In 1776, Paine wrote *Common Sense*, helped fuel the separation of America from Great Britain. He then served as a soldier in the American Revolution. He returned to England in 1787, and then went to France in 1792 as a supporter of the French Revolution. In 1794, he published his *Age of Reason*, the deistic work, brought him much criticism from his former American friends. Upon his return to America in 1802, he found no welcome and eventually died as an outcast.)

Thomas Paine on "The Study of God" delivered in Paris on January 16, 1797, in a discourse to the Society of Theophilanthropists.

The words of Thomas Paine [express disapproval of the U.S. government school system]:

It has been the error of the schools to teach astronomy, and all the other sciences and subjects of natural philosophy, as accomplishments only; whereas they should be taught theologically, or with reference to the Being who is the author of them: for all the principles of science are of Divine origin. Man cannot make, or invent, or contrive principles. He can only discover them; and he ought to look through the discovery to the Author.

When we examine an extraordinary piece of machinery, an astonishing pile of architecture, a well executed statue or a highly finished painting where life and action are imitated, and habit only prevents our mistaking a surface of light and shade for cubical solidity, our ideas are naturally led to think of the extensive genius and talents of the artist. When we study the elements of geometry, we think of Euclid. When we speak of gravitation, we think of Newton. How then is it, that when we study the works of God in the creation, we stop short, and do not think of God? It is from the error of the schools in having taught those subjects as accomplishments only, and thereby separated the study of them from the Being who is the author of them. . . .

The evil that has resulted from the error of the schools in teaching natural philosophy as an accomplishment only has been that of generating in the pupils a species of atheism. Instead of looking through the works of the creation to the Creator himself, they stop short, and employ the knowledge

they acquire to create doubts of His existence. They labor with studied ingenuity to ascribe everything they behold to innate properties of matter; and jump over all the rest, by saying that matter is eternal.

(http://www.wallbuilders.com/LIBissuesArticles.asp?id=81) David Barton, Wall Builders

SOCIALISM AND THE CHURCH

When I write of the church and socialism, I am referring, of course, to the church in the abstract. Thank God, there are still a few true churches in America.

A few decades ago, the great preacher from Wales, the Reverend Doctor Martyn Lloyd-Jones (1919-1981)[45] preached a message entitled, "The state of the nation." His text was taken from Psalm 11:3 in the authorized version, "If the foundations be destroyed, what can the righteous do?"

We live in a day of denial of all moral principles. There have been many times in the past of great wickedness and immorality. However, today we live in a time when many of our people are not merely immoral, they are amoral. We can hardly call upon people to repent if their method of epistemology does not acknowledge the fruit of sin and a Divine authority.

Although the true Marxist denies all forms of religion he realized in America he must subvert and work through religion to establish the socialist nation that we have become. The church must share with the novelist, the movie industry, television, and the news media for the grim condition of America.

Dr. R. J. Rushdoony remarked, "The beginning of true liberty is Jesus Christ. And therefore the first and last target of all subversion is Biblical faith. Hence it is that the church has been the first target in infiltration and subversion: and is the most subverted institution in the United States today."

---

[45] Dr. Lloyd-Jones was both a medical doctor and a graduate of seminary.

We did not arrive in our present situation overnight. The abolitionists of the middle of the nineteenth century were mostly Unitarians and Transcendentalists. They were recognized by Dr. James H. Thornwell, The *New York Herald*, R. L. Dabney, and others as being socialists.

Theodore Parker, a friend of Horace Mann, and a member of the "secret six" who financed the terrorist activities of old John Brown, had socialistic views. He was an eloquent Transcendentalist preacher and a rabid abolitionist. The Marxian view of religion is quite apparent in this excerpt from Theodore Parker's "A Sermon on Merchants," preached in 1846:

> Now the merchants in America occupy the place was once held by the fighters and next by the nobles . . . In virtue of its strength and position this class is the controlling one in politics . . . your congress is its marrow. This class is the controlling one in churches . . . in the same way it buys up the clergymen . . . the clergymen will do its work, putting them in comfortable places. The merchants build mainly the churches and endow theological schools; they furnish material sinews of the church. Hence metropolitan churches are in general as much commercial as shops . . .This class owns the machinery of society in great measure, the ships, factories, ships, water privileges, houses and the like. This brings into their employment large masses of workingmen, with no capital but muscles and skill.[46]

The influence of Unitarian and Transcendental heresies infected the thinking and the theology of several mainline denominations in the North to such an extent that the Bible believing churches in the

---

[46] Gary Lee Roper, *Antebellum Slavery: An Orthodox Christian View*, 113.

South could no longer fellowship with them. The Presbyterian Church split in 1938. The Methodists in the South broke with their Northern counterparts in 1844. In 1845, the Southern Baptist Convention was formed. The Episcopal Church split at the beginning of the War.

I do not hereby imply that there were no orthodox churches left in the North but merely that the church can be penetrated and undermined as we shall see when we examine the National Council of Churches.

It is rather surprising that a well educated conservative would list Charles Grandison Finney (1792-1875) in the Christian Hall of Fame. This is exactly what Elmer L. Towns did, however. Finney, the abolitionist, <u>is the father of the Social Gospel</u>.[47] Although ordained as a Presbyterian minister, he did not accept the Westminster Confession of Faith and later did have the decency to withdraw from the Presbyterians. His ministry was man-centered, not God-centered. Finney in giving account of his conversion repeats over and over again about what HE did. However, it is apparent that God did nothing.

When Charles Grandison Finney gave an account of his conversion experiences we find these expressions: **I** told the Lord . . . **my** intellect . . . the **voluntary** powers of **my** mind . . . **I** seized hold of them . . . **my** conviction . . . **my** mind . . . **I** just accepted it."

Evidently God did not do anything in his conversion. In real conversion God, like the great potter takes a piece of worthless clay, puts it upon the potter's wheel, turns it, cuts it, and molds it

---

[47] Many present day historians refer to Dr. Walter Rauschenbusch as the "father of the Social Gospel." This Marxist was a leader in the subversion of the Christian church in America.

into a vessel for His glory. If you tell me that you have been converted show me the evidence that God has done something!

In St. Matthew 5:20 our Lord said; " . . .*That except your righteousness shall exceed the righteousness of the scribes and Pharisees, ye shall in no case enter into the kingdom of heaven."*

Today we do not think highly of the scribes and Pharisees but during our Lord's earthly ministry the Jews had a saying, "if only two men get to heaven, one will be a scribe and the other a Pharisee.

Evidently though, there was something seriously and fatally defective in their righteousness. This great defect can be seen in the passage from St. Luke 18:10-14: *"Two men went up into the temple to pray; the one a Pharisee, and the other a publican. The Pharisee stood and prayed thus with himself, God, I thank thee that I am not as other men are, extortioners, unjust, adulterers, or even as this publican. I fast twice in the week, I give tithes of all that I possess. And the publican, standing afar off, would not lift up so much as his eyes unto heaven, but smote upon his breast, saying, God be merciful to me a sinner. I tell you, this man went down to his house justified rather than the other; for every one that exalteth himself shall be abased; and he that humbleth himself shall be exalted."*

The fault in the Pharisees prayer is easily ascertained in this passage. The essence of what he said was, "What I am and what I do commends me to God."

How often do we hear similar testimony, I went to church and listen to the preaching. I decided for Christ. I went forward to the front and shook the preacher's hand. I was baptized and joined the church. Now, I read the Bible, and I tithe. I have reformed.

> "I don't drink, cuss, nor chew, nor run around with them that do."

This is all essentially the righteousness of the scribes and Pharisees and that will not get one into heaven. I like the testimony in what the contemporary worshipers call one of those "stale old hymns."

> "My hope is built on nothing less than Jesus' blood and righteousness, I dare not trust the sweetest frame, but wholly lean on Jesus' name."[48]

Finney was the inventor of the modern invitation system. According to him, man could come to Christ without the power of the Holy Spirit. He equated the "physical movement" of walking the aisle the equivalent of the "spiritual movement" of coming to Christ. In this he revealed his Semi-Pelagianism.

The gospel preached by Charles Finney was not the old gospel preached by Jonathan Edwards, George Whitefield, or C. H. Spurgeon. The exhortation of modern evangelists to "decide for Christ" is misleading. I may decide that I will not like ice cream anymore, but unless God changes my taste buds, I will still crave it.

An excellent description between the old gospel and the new gospel is given by J. I Packer in the Introductory Essay to John Owens's book, the *Death of Death* in the "Death of Christ." Packer remarks concerning the old gospel:

---

[48] "The Solid Rock," lyrics by Edward Mote (1797-1874); music by William B. Bradley (1816-1868).

It is not likely, therefore, that a preacher of the old gospel will be happy to express the application of it in the form of a demand to "decide for Christ," as the current phrase is. For, on the one hand, this phrase carries the wrong associations. It suggests voting a person into office—an act in which the candidate plays no part beyond offering himself for election, and everything then being settled by the voter's independent choice. But we do not vote God's Son into office as our Savior, nor does He remain passive while preachers campaign on His behalf, whipping up support for His cause. We ought not to think of evangelism as a kind of electioneering. And then on the other hand, this phrase obscures the very thing that is essential in repentance and faith—the denying of self in a personal approach to Christ. It is not at all obvious that deciding for Christ is the same as coming to Him and resting on Him and turning from sin and self-effort; it sounds like something much less, and is accordingly calculated to instill defective notions of what the gospel really requires of sinners. It is not a very apt phrase from any point of view.

The Marxist minister, Walter Rauschenbusch, declared, "If Socialism is to succeed, it cannot succeed in an irreligious country. It must start in the churches."

The present National Council of Churches (NCC) was formed in 1950 by a merger of the Federal Council of Churches formed in 1908 and other left-wing ecumenical organizations. Thirty-three denominations were originally represented. In 1932, the Federal Council, (FCC) was formally branded as subversive by Congressional Committee Report Number 2290.

The ultimate goal of Marxist controlled organization of churches was the establishment of a One World Government, One World Religion, and One World Race.

The Wise Man said, *The thing that hath been, it [is that] which shall be; and that which is done [is] that which shall be done: and [there is] no new [thing] under the sun.* Ecclesiastes 1:9

After the great flood God divided the descendants of Noah into nations (Genesis 10:32). At that time the whole earth was of one language and God intended for them to disperse upon the earth. Nimrod, a type of the anti-Christ, rebelled against God's plan because he wanted to be the master of a One World Government, a One World Religion, and a One World Race.

God was displeased with Nimrod's plan and said, ". . . *Behold, the people is one . . . So the Lord scattered them abroad from thence upon the face of all the earth."* (Genesis 11:6, 8).

And then we read in Acts 17:26 that God, ". . . *hath made of one blood all nations of men for to dwell on all the face of the earth, and hath determined the times before appointed, and the bounds of their habitation."*

According to Strong's *Concordance*, the word, "nations" in Acts 17:26 could have been translated "races."

Evidently God did not think highly of diversity and He was certainly against Globalism and the ONE WORLD advocated by the National Council of Churches, the United Nations, the Council of Foreign Relations (CFR) and the International Bankers.

The National Council of Churches has completely denounced Orthodox Christianity and has from its very formation been dedicated to the overthrow of capitalism and constitutional government and devoted to the promotion of communism.

Apostasy of the Church

The National Council of Churches

The beginning of true liberty is Jesus Christ. And therefore the first and last target of all subversion is biblical faith. Hence it is that the Church has been the first target of infiltration and subversion; and is the most subverted institution in the United States today.

—Dr. R. J. Rushdoony

David Emerson Gumaer spent two years within the youth apparatus of the Communist Party as an undercover operative for Chicago Police Intelligence. In December of 1967 he accepted the invitation of the Senate Internal Security Subcommittee to testify in executive session regarding his knowledge of the activities and personnel of the W.E.B. Dubois Clubs and the Students for a Democratic Society. Mr. Gumaer is currently a Contributing Editor to The Review of the News *(an outstanding new national newsweekly) and has lectured widely.*

Claiming to speak with authority for some 42 million American Christians, the National Council of the Churches of Christ (N.C.C.) includes thirty-three denominations representing most of the major Protestant and Orthodox Churches in the United States. In addition, more than a score of denominations not actually members of the N.C.C. have participated actively in its radical programs.

Headquartered at 475 Riverside Drive in New York City, the National Council functions through dozens of interlocking departments, grouped under four major divisions, overseeing the N.C.C.'s international operations. The program is of such magnitude that in 1968, alone, the National Council of Churches expended over $19 million on a worldwide network of Leftist projects. In that year, however, the N.C.C. *collected* $24,819,000 from gullible American Christians and tax-exempt Leftist foundations.

During the meeting of this group's General Assembly at San Diego in February of 1968, a presentation titled "NCC Ministries and the Communist World" revealed that in 1967 over $1,584,000 had been given to the Communist Government of Poland through an N.C.C. on-going ministry called Church World Service. Although the aid was received in the name of the Polish Ecumenical Council, it was administered by the Communists for their own purposes. During the period from 1952 until 1967, over $40 million worth of food, clothing, and other material was give by the N.C.C.'s Church World Service to the Communist Government of Yugoslavia. Even stranger was an admission in this N.C.C. report that the National Council was operating a "refugee program" picked up the tab for relocating Brazilian Communists in Mexico.

To top it off, in 1968 the same U.S. Government prohibits prayer in our schools donated $5 million to the National Council of Churches through something called "Ocean Freight Refunds." In fact, in its 1960 triennial report, the N.C.C. lists "Ocean Freight Refunds" from the federal government totaling more than $23 million for the period 1957 to 1960.

The recipient of this federal largesse is the same National Council of Churches whose 1968 General Assembly at San Diego demanded that America:

"Stop the bombing of North Vietnam as a prelude to seeking a negotiated peace"; "Avoid *provocative*

military actions against Communist China in the knowledge that it has a legitimate interest in Asia"; "Press for the admission of the Peking government to the United Nations"; "Create conditions for cooperation between the United States and the Communist countries of Eastern Europe, the Soviet Union and Cuba"; "Recognize the government of Cuba and acknowledge the existence of the East German Republic"; and, "Remove restrictions on imports from Communist countries and on cultural exchanges between the U.S. and the Soviet Union."

Other resolutions called for "increased support for poverty-rights action groups by Church Women United," and provided for financial backing of the subversive National Urban Coalition. The N.C.C. even directed its member churches "to provide funds for local black groups to strategize for the summer and to support inclusion of black power and black nationalist organizations in local task groups...." In other words, the resolutions of the National Council exactly followed the current Communist Line.

The N.C.C. has consistently propagandized for every conceivable Leftist program, from federally forced integration to complete disarmament of the United States. From its office in Washington, D.C., the National Council's spokesmen regularly appear before Committees of Congress to lobby for the causes of the Far Left, though the National Council has never registered under the Lobbying Act of 1946. And, despite its having been repeatedly exposed as a fraud the N.C.C. has somehow continued to maintain not only its reputation for legitimacy, but its tax-exempt status as well. It is very well shielded indeed, and rooted in a conspiracy against Christianity in America goes back more than eighty years.

A full decade before the turn of the century, the seeds of the Marxist "social gospel" were already being planted within our major seminaries and divinity schools by returning American theologians who had studied in England and Germany. There they had become infected with the virus of a Conspiracy had already changed much of the spiritual and moral structure of Europe. After awhile, of course, America produced her own clerical conspirators. One of these was a man named Walter Rauschenbusch.

In 1885, Rauschenbusch was graduated from the prestigious Rochester Theological Seminary, thoroughly indoctrinated in the Socialist tenets of "Illumanism" — a philosophy calling itself a religion but substituting faith in man for faith in God. As the atheist Karl Marx noted: "Illumanism is really nothing else but Marxism." Rauschenbusch was both a Illumanist and a Marxist. Thus, in 1892 he and a group of Comrades organized "The Brotherhood of the Kingdom" to promote their radical beliefs along Fabian lines. Walter Rauschenbusch declared: "If ever Socialism is to succeed, it cannot succeed in an irreligious country. It must start in the churches."

And start in the churches it did.

In New York, the Reverend F.D. Huntington — another Marxist — was busy founding the American branch of the Christian Socialist Movement. It was to be a religious arm of the infamous Fabian Socialist Society had been created some years earlier in London at the direction of Sidney and Beatrice Webb, George Bernard Shaw, and a host of other prominent Marxists of the time. Indeed, the Webbs made a trip to the United States in 1898 to review the success of Fabian infiltration of religion. By the turn of the century, Marxist plans for the capture of our churches were proceeding apace.

In February of 1900 the first effort to create a National Federation of Churches resulted in a nationwide committee of twenty-five leading churchmen, many of whom were devoted Fabians. One of those young organizers was an English protégé of Walter Rauschenbusch named Harry F. Ward. Years later, in sworn testimony before the House Committee on Un-American Activities, it would be revealed that Ward was not only a secret Communist, but "the Red Dean of the Communist Party in the religious field."

By February 1901, delegates from local church federations met at Philadelphia and formed the National Federation of Churches, forerunner of a larger, more powerful Fabian organization whose projects on behalf of the Communist apparatus would radically alter the course of American history. The next year at Chicago, during the national convention of the Socialist Party, a number of prominent N.F.C. clergymen participated actively.

There followed a Committee on Correspondence, made up of the more radical ministers and laymen of the day, toured the nation's seminaries and church offices propagandizing for yet another Red project, an Inter-Church Conference on Federation. Deliberations at that important Conference, held in New York on November 15, 1905, would have a profound influence on the minds and actions of thousands of religious leaders for many years to come. It was at that historic gathering that the first formal proposal was made calling for the formation of the Federal Council of Churches, now the National Council of Churches.

In 1907 the Far Left created a supporting Front called the Methodist Federation for Social Service, a "religious" organization found by the House Committee on Un-American Activities to have been a key apparatus of the Communist Conspiracy since its very inception.[1]
In fact, when it was finally exposed years later, it was cited as "Among the more Conspicuous fronts for Communist activity . . . "And, as you might expect, one of the founding Methodist ministers was Harry F. Ward, the brilliant protégé of Walter Rauschenbusch. For the next thirty-five years this Communist Front was directed

by Comrade Ward, and staffed by numerous functionaries of the Communist Party.

By this time the groundwork had been laid and Dr. Rauschenbusch paid a return visit to Sidney and Beatrice Webb in England, fully committing himself to Fabian designs for subversion of the Christian church in America. The following year, on December 2, 1908, Waller Rauschenbusch and Harry Ward set up a nine-day conference at Philadelphia during the Federal Council of Churches of Christ in America (F.C.C.) was officially formed by representatives of twenty-nine Protestant and Eastern Orthodox denominations. The F.C.C. then chose as its constitution the same plan of federation that had earlier been adopted by the Socialists attending the 1905 Inter-Church Conference on Federation. They also adopted "The Social Creed of the Churches" written by English Communist Harry F. Ward, who had earlier submitted his Plan to Nikolai Lenin for approval.

By 1914 the Federal Council of Churches had become one of the major outlets in America for Marxist propaganda. On February tenth of that year a group of conspirators met in the home of millionaire industrialist Andrew Carnegie and laid plans for something called the Church Peace Union. In *Pioneers For Peace Through Religion,* Charles S. MacFarland (at the time General Secretary of the F.C.C.) reveals that this group included only those religious leaders who were in some way connected with the Federal Council of Churches. This newly formed organization was the brainchild of top conspirator Andrew Carnegie, who used it to capture for the *Insiders* the controlling clique of the Federal Council by subsidizing the Church Peace Union to the tune of $2 million.

Shortly after the meeting with Carnegie, two international church conferences were promoted by the F.C.C.'s Church Peace Union — one for Roman Catholics, to be held at Liegé, Belgium, and the other for

Protestants at Constance, Germany. Both were scheduled to convene on August 1, 1914. , by an odd "coincidence," was the very day that war was declared between Germany and Russia.

Several months later, at Cambridge in England, the Fabian Socialists set up an International Fellowship of Reconciliation to protest the War while propagandizing for Socialism. This was followed a year later on November 11, 1915, by the formation of an American Branch of F.O.R., organized by such stalwarts of the Federal Council of Churches as Harry F. Ward and Walter Rauschenbusch. They were aided in this project by leading Socialists **Norman Thomas, Oswald Garrison Villard**[49], and **Jane Addams** (at whose home in Chicago the Webbs stayed during their visit to America). **In April 1917, one month after the Czar had been forced to surrender control of his government to Socialist Alexander Kerensky, The United States was finally maneuvered into World War I, thus ending 141 years of neutrality.** That fall, a relative handful of Bolsheviks led by Nikolai Lenin captured the Government of Russia, thereby establishing a base for the Marxists' continuing world revolution.

By 1918, as its interlock with the Fellowship of Reconciliation became more pronounced, the Federal Council of Churches stepped up its agitation against the War and became the major propagandist in America for the Bolshevik Revolution. That year, too, with the passing of **Walter Rauschenbusch**, the mantle of the Marxist movement within the church passed to Comrade **Harry Ward**, who had by then begun teaching the Red dialectic at Union Theological Seminary, where he was to remain for twenty-five years.

In early 1919 the Russian Communists issued a call for the founding of the Communist International, resulting

---

[49] Grandson of rabid abolitionist William Lloyd Garrison who advocated murder of slaveholders.

that September first in the formation of the American Communist Party from the Left wing of the Socialist Party. Among the hundreds of delegates at the founding convention in Chicago were Comrades John Keracher and Dennis Batt, representing the Michigan State organization of the Socialist Party. They insisted "that the Communist Party should in its program adopt a plan calling for an all-out campaign against religion as its main and immediate objective." Years later a charter member of the Party revealed:

The policy in those days was framed in such a way that the members of the Communist Party could infiltrate church organizations for the purpose of conducting their propaganda among them, for enlisting their support for Soviet Russia, and for the various campaigns in which the Communists were interested.

In the early twenties the Communist Party made considerable gains in its program to infiltrate the churches. This effort was led by such prominent "American" clergymen as Harry F. Ward, Jerome Davis, William B. Spofford, and Albert Rhys Williams. As former top Communist Benjamin Gitlow told the House Committee on Un-American Activities in 1953: "This group wielded tremendous influence in the religious field and did Trojan Horse work in advancing the Communist conspiracy in religion."

The most important Communist in the field of religion, said Gitlow, was Robert W. Dunn — who "served as the Communist Party's liaison between its political committee and secretariat and the clergymen operating under instructions of the Party." Comrade Dunn, an official with the American Civil Liberties Union, carried his orders to Harry Ward and the others, who in turn issued directives of their own. Comrades Ward, Spofford, Davis, and Williams were all leaders of the F.C.C. and all were members of the Communist Party. Williams even worked in the Soviet Union as an assistant in the Commissariat of Foreign Affairs.

In **1922** the American Communist Party, and all Communist Parties throughout the world, adopted the "United Front" strategy ordered by Nikolai Lenin and the Communist International. This enabled the Reds greatly to expand their infiltration of religion. As Ben Gitlow testified: **"The number of clergymen who followed the Communist Party line grew by leaps and bounds."**

In 1924 (and again in 1929) Federal Council chieftain Harry Ward traveled to Moscow to discuss with Stalin the use of the churches in furthering the goals of the International Communist Conspiracy. In early 1925, Ward was sent to China where he lectured widely among Christian clergymen. His lectures in China were discussed at length at the Comintern, and it was agreed that "the missions and church institutions in China could be used . . . to cover up Communist espionage activities. . . . "That was also the case in this country, where the Federal Council already had a budget of $350,000 and an office in Washington from it promoted Communist interests.

In 1927 the F.C.C.'s lobbying for Communist causes became so flagrant that Congressman Arthur M. Free introduced a resolution in the House of Representatives describing the Federal Council as "a communist organization aimed at the establishment of a state-church.... "In that same year, a report issued by the Military Intelligence Association branded the F.C.C. as subversive. Another denunciation appeared in the Naval Institute Proceedings of 1928, which established that the Federal Council had been meddling in defense matters and was "probably the most powerful propaganda organization in the country."

Testifying before the Senate Lobbying Investigating Committee, Congressman George Tinkham revealed that he had received propaganda from the F.C.C. on fifteen different political issues. Tinkham later revealed that *Insider* John D. Rockefeller Jr. had from 1926 to 1929 contributed over $137,000 to the Federal Council of Churches — a sum equal to about ten percent of its total annual income from all sources.

During 1932 the Federal Council suffered a series of setbacks. Congressional Committee Report Number *2290* formally branded the F.C.C. as subversive. And the *Sunday School Times* of August 13, 1932, exposed an obscene F.C.C. sex manual entitled *Young People's Relationships,* described as "a crowning achievement of the Federal Council controlling group along the line of preparing the way for atheistic Communism." Also, Major Amos A. Fries produced documentation before a Hearing of the House Immigration Committee in January 1932, proving that "There has been an interlocking board of directorates all the way from the Federal Council of Churches to the most extreme Communists."

During this hectic period for the F.C.C., Harry Ward was graduating one of his more interesting protégés from Union Theological Seminary in New York — an eager young Marxist who promptly began working for the A.C.L.U. Ward's pupil was Arnold Johnson, now Public Relations Director for the Communist Party, U.S.A. The following year Comrade Johnson served as Field Secretary for the Communists National Religion and Labor Foundation, created in 1932 by Communist Sidney Hillman. Acting in the same capacity as Johnson in that effort was Willard E. Uphaus, a Federal Council official who has since affiliated himself with ten other officially cited Communist projects. Other F.C.C. officials listed on the letterhead of the Reds' National Religion and Labor Foundation include such members of its Executive Committee as Communists Jerome Davis, A.J. Muste, and Charles C. Webber.

By 1935 Communist infiltration of religion in the United States was in full swing, presaging orders of the Seventh World Conference of the Comintern at Moscow to maintain such subversion. On September 10, 1935, a

Report on the F.C.C. from the Office of Naval Intelligence was read into the *Congressional Record,* establishing that the Federal Council was one of several organizations "give aid and comfort to the Communist movement and Party." Its leadership, the Intelligence Report revealed, "consists of a small radical group dictates its policy," and "it is always extremely active in any matter against national defense." In fact the Chief of Naval Operations, Admiral William H. Standley, formally accused the F.C.C. of collaborating with the Communists.

How far the Federal Council of Churches was prepared to go in pushing the Communist Line was revealed in a special report issued by the Commission to Study the Bases of a Just and Durable Peace, at the 1942 convention of the F.C.C. It called for:

Ultimately, "a world *government of delegated powers." Complete abandonment of U.S. isolationism. Strong immediate limitations on national sovereignty. International control of all armies and navies. A universal system of money.... Worldwide freedom of immigration. Progressive elimination of all tariff and quota restrictions on world trade .... A "democratically controlled" international bank ....*

Chairman of the Commission issued these proposals was John Foster Dulles, an *Insider* who was a leader of the Federal Council of Churches.

The F.C.C. conference concluded:

Many duties now performed by local and national governments "can now be effectively carried out only by international authority." Individual nations . . . must give up their armed forces "except for preservation of domestic order" and allow the world to be policed by an international army and navy ....

Three years later, in 1945, the Federal Council of Churches was one of only forty-two non-governmental organizations invited to send delegates to the international conference at San Francisco founded the United Nations. Presiding over the U.N. conclave was Communist agent Alger Hiss, who like Dulles had earlier served as Chairman of an important committee of the Federal Council of Churches. The Federal Council even boasted that it had first conceived the idea of the United Nations, and noted that one of its prominent officials, John Foster Dulles, had been responsible for incorporating the Federal Council's "Six Pillars of Peace" into the U.N. Charter.

Nonetheless, the F.C.C. had taken quite a beating from Conservatives during the Forties. It was time for a change of image if it was to survive. On November 29, 1950, the Federal Council held a convention at Cleveland where it absorbed four additional agencies (the Church World Service, the Inter-seminary Committee, the Protestant Film Commission, and the Protestant Radio Commission), and formally changed its name to the National Council of the Churches of Christ in the U.S.A. Leaders of the old Marxist organization became leaders in the new one. In fact, the F.C.C.'s *Bulletin* that December explained: "All the work of the Federal Council will continue under new auspices....other divisions of the National Council and the general administration of the Council will also draw upon the resources in both personnel and finances."

In checking the quick-change artistry of the Federal Council of Churches, Dr. J.B. Mathews, who compiled the voluminous *Appendix IX* of the Dies Committee on Un-American Activities, found:

In the formal constitution of the National Council of Churches in Cleveland, one representative from each of the participating denominations signed the official book became the Document of Record. Eleven of these 29 signers of the official book have public records of affiliation with pro-Communist enterprises....

There were 358 clergymen who were voting delegates to the constituting convention.... Of these clergymen, 123 (or 34 per cent) have had affiliations with Communist projects and enterprises. That represents a high degree of Communist penetration.[2]

The overlap between the old Council and the new was almost complete. It included Edwin T. Dahlberg who had been Chairman of the Department of Evangelism in the F.C.C. and later became President of the "new" National Council of Churches. The public record shows that Dahlberg has affiliated himself with at least twenty-seven officially cited Communist projects. Bishop G. Bromley Oxnam, who had been President of the F.C.C. in 1948, became a member of the powerful N.C.C. General Board. Oxnam has a record of affiliations with forty-one officially cited Communist Fronts and projects. Roswell P. Barnes, as Associate General Secretary of the F.C.C. in 1940, and editor of the F.C.C. *Bulletin* in later years, turned up as Executive Secretary of the N.C.C.'s Division of Christian Life and Work. Barnes has associated himself with nine officially cited Communist Fronts. And then there was Walter W. Van Kirk, who had held the identical title of Executive Director of both the F.C.C. and N.C.C. Department of International Justice and Goodwill. The list, as one might expect, could go on and on.

What is most interesting about control of the National Council of Churches is that its hierarchy consists of a General Assembly made up of 750 delegates who meet once every three years. From this group is chosen a General Board of 275 members who meet every four months. The rules provide that a quorum must be present to take any official action, and that a majority of those present must be in favor of said action for it to be official. The fantastic thing about this is that it only takes 20 of the 275 to constitute a quorum — and a majority of that twenty is *eleven*. Therefore, the balance of power lies in the hands of just eleven men who can issue a declaration on any political subject and promulgate that declaration in the name of thirty-three denominations comprising over 42 million American Protestants. That, people, is just the way the Communists want it.

In 1951, opposition to the N.C.C. came from both the House Committee on Un-American Activities (see its investigation of the Communist Committee for Peaceful Alternatives to the Atlantic Pact), and from a newly formed Methodist organization based in Cincinnati, the anti-Communist "Circuit Riders."

The year 1952 began with the H.C.U.A. exposing the Communists' Methodist Federation for Social Action, was found to be directly linked to both the F.C.C. and the successor N.C.C. The House Committee also heard testimony from former Communist leader Joseph Kornfeder, who said there were at that time somewhere in the neighborhood of 600 American clergymen who were members of the Communist Party. Kornfeder had trained at the Lenin School of Political Warfare in Moscow from 1927 to 1930, been a top aide of Josef Stalin, and spoke from experience.

When Dwight Eisenhower took office, Leftists in the National Council of Churches began to pop up in key posts in the Administration. There was John Foster Dulles, who became Secretary of State; Harold Stassen, who became Mutual Security Director (he had been Vice President of the N.C.C. and President of its International Council of Religious Education); and, Arthur S. Flemming, who became head of the manpower division of the Department of Defense and later Secretary of Health, Education and Welfare.[3] President Eisenhower personally added prestige to the N.C.C. by speaking at its functions.

During 1953 the Senate Internal Security Subcommittee and the House Committee on Un-American Activities took thousands of pages of testimony on Communist penetration of all phases of American life. In July of that year, H.C.U.A. heard testimony from such former leaders of the Communist Party as Manning Johnson, Benjamin Gitlow, and Joseph Kornfeder, detailing

Communist infiltration and manipulation of our nation's churches. Supporting evidence was likewise given in sworn testimony by such experts as former Communists Paul Crouch, Karl Prussion, and Albert Vassart. The latter testified that "In 1936, Moscow sent out an order to have sure and carefully selected Communist youth enter the seminaries and become priests." After all, Stalin had himself been a seminarian.

1953 was also the year of the famous G. Bromley Oxnam Hearing before the House Committee on Un-American Activities, in Oxnam admitted his participation in numerous Communist projects and implicated his N.C.C. Comrades. During that year the American Legion launched a drive to block the N.C.C. effort to bypass the McCarran Act in order to bring Communist clergymen to America from the Soviet Bloc. Meanwhile, the National Council was attacking the Bricker Amendment and the McCarren-Walter Internal Security Act of 1950.

The following year, while the National Council of Churches was pushing to abolish Bible reading in public schools, Walter Reuther presented a check to the N.C.C. for $200,000 — a grant from the C.I.O.'s Philip Murray Memorial Foundation. In the meantime, the Communist *Daily Worker* was devoting its space to reporting the National Council's attacks on Senator Joseph McCarthy and on all Congressional Committees investigating subversive activities.

In 1958 the National Council of Churches World Order Study Conference met at Cleveland, Ohio, from November eighteenth through the twenty-first. As the Communist *Worker* reported, the Cleveland delegates proposed:

Diplomatic recognition by the United States of Red China — and its admission to the United Nations; Co-existence with "the Communist nations"; Avoidance of "the posture of general hostility" to "the Communist nations"; Ratification of the genocide convention;

Internationalism to supersede national patriotism; "Disarmament by multilateral agreement" for "universal disarmament"; "The creation of a permanent United Nations police force" and abolition of universal military training; "Abolition of the system of military conscription" and of the Selective Service System; Extension of trade and travel without restriction between the United States and Communist countries.

Of course, these N.C.C. proposals might just as well have come directly from Moscow. We are told, however, that they emanated from a "Message to the Churches," prepared by a committee of twenty-three N.C.C. laymen and clergy under the chairmanship of Dr. John C. Bennett, dean of the faculty at Union Theological Seminary. As one would assume, Bennett had already affiliated himself with at least twenty-seven officially cited Communist Fronts and projects.

What is most interesting about the Cleveland Conference is that, of the six hundred delegates, two-thirds were laymen. The Circuit Riders note in *Recognize Red China?* that one-half of the registered clergymen at the conference, or 103, had public records of affiliation with Communist Fronts and causes.

The next major incident to jar the hierarchy of the National Council came on February 25, 1960, with the publication of *Issues Presented by Air Reserve Center Training Manual,* a Report of the House Committee on Un-American Activities. As the H.C.U.A. Report revealed, the Air Force had issued a training manual for its officers dealt at some length with Communist penetration of religion. Officials of the National Council of Churches, learning of this, immediately contacted Secretary of the Air Force Dudley C. Sharp, demanding that this "offensive" manual be removed and the chapter pertaining to subversion of religion be rewritten to exclude any mention of Communist penetration. On the same day that the N.C.C. message was received, February 11, 1960, General Lloyd P. Hopwood, Director of Personnel Procurement and Training of the U.S. Air Force, ordered the manual withdrawn.

Some time thereafter, Secretary of Defense Thomas Gates told the Press: "in response to the letter of the National Council of Churches... I have assured this fine organization of my very genuine regrets regarding the statement that appeared in [*the*] Air Force Reserve Manual .... "

Citing the "offensive" passage on page fifty-three of the *Air Reserve Center Training Manual,* H.C.U.A. staff director Richard Arens quoted it as follows:

A while back Americans were shocked to find that Communists had infiltrated our churches....

The Communist Party, U.S.A., has instructed many of its members to join churches and church groups, to take control whenever possible, and to influence the thoughts and actions of as many church-goers as they can .... The party tries to get leading church men to support Communist policies disguised as welfare work for minorities. Earl Browder, former head of the American Communist party, once admitted: "By going among the religious masses, we are for the first time able to bring our anti-religious ideas to them."

Are there Communist Ministers? Sure.

The manual then named two such identified Communist ministers — the Reverend Eliot While, and the Reverend Claude C. Williams. It was Williams who once boasted: "Denominationally I am a Presbyterian, religiously a Unitarian, and politically I am a Communist. I am not preaching to make people good or anything of the sort, I'm in the church because I can reach people easier that way and get them organized for Communism."

Defending the H.C.U.A. position favoring the unaltered Air Force Reserve Manual, staff director Arens declared:

...in view of the Secretary's repudiation of the information conveyed respecting the National Council of

Churches of Christ in America, the chairman issued a statement to the effect that the leadership of the [N.C.C.] *had hundreds or at least over a hundred affiliations with Communist fronts and causes. Since then we have made careful, but yet incomplete checks, and it is a complete understatement. Thus far of the leadership of the National Council of Churches of Christ in America, we have found over 100 persons leadership capacity with either Communist-front records or records of service to Communists causes. The aggregate affiliations of the leadership, instead of being in the hundreds as the* [H.C.U.A.] *chairman. first indicated, is now, according to our latest count, into the thousands, and we have yet to complete our check....*

Another matter raised by the *Air Reserve Center Training Manual* was the fact that on September 30, 1952, the National Council of Churches had published a "Revised Standard Version" of the Bible in many beloved passages were altered, and adulterated phrases substituted to fit the social gospel of the N.C.C. Of the ninety translators named in a brochure issued by the N.C.C. at least thirty have been affiliated with ninety major Communist Fronts or projects.

Several months later, on April 20, 1960, Congressman Donald Jackson read into the Congressional *Record* (Pages 7842-7846) a shocking exposé of the pamphlet *The Negro American: A Reading List,* published in 1957 by the Department of Racial and Cultural Relations of the National Council of Churches. This pamphlet was a bibliography of 260 books on "Negro history," many of had been written by identified Communists. The Foreword to that reading list, by Alfred S. Kramer, slated: "We of the National Council. . . consider ... these books ... safe to recommend for children." Among the Communist authors recommended were: Victor Perlo, former head of a Soviet espionage ring operating within the U.S. government; Herbert Aptheker, chief theoretician for the Communist Party, U.S.A.; W.E.B. DuBois, an admitted Communist in whose honor the

Party later named its youth affiliate; Shirley Graham, DuBois' Communist wife (who was in charge of all radio and television propaganda in Ghana when it was controlled by the Communists); and, Langston Hughes, whose blasphemous poem, "Goodbye Christ," scrapes the bottom in Communist sacrilege (Hughes had nine books on that reading list). A committee of ten clergy and laymen, headed by Dr. J. Oscar Lee (an N.C.C. Executive Director), had approved this N.C.C. reading list.

Obviously we will not be able to go into many more of the hundreds of subversive operations of the National Council of Churches because of limitations on our space. But, ever so briefly, let us touch on a few additional items of major importance.

On June 7, 1963, the N.C.C. created an Emergency Commission on Religion and Race headed by Dr. Martin Luther King, Walter Reuther, and Eugene Carson Blake. It was a Major coalition of Leftist forces run by Dr. Robert W. Spike, who after successfully leading the attack on the South during the N.C.C.'s Delta Project was murdered at Columbus, Ohio, in 1966 in circumstances led police to believe that he had been a practicing pervert. Lewd pictures of homosexuals, names and addresses of known deviates, and addresses of homosexual hangouts in several cities were found in his possession.

Working with Spike in that N.C.C. Delta Project (included the Reds' march on Selma, Alabama, in 1965) were Bayard Rustin, a convicted sexual deviate and former organizer for the Young Communist League; Myles Horton, Marxist director of the notorious Highlander Folk School; and, the Delta Ministry's associate director, the Reverend Warren McKenna. The Reverend McKenna was photographed in 1957, sitting during a visit to Red China with Communist Premier Chou En-lai, and has been referred to by Herbert Philbrick (in a government document called *Communist*

Passport Frauds) as "one of the leading collaborators of, and apologists for, the Soviet Union."

In March and April of 1964 the Communist *Worker* announced an N.C.C. coalition to create a March on Washington — a march officially designated as a project of the Communists Party.

Then there is the Sixth Triennial Conference of the National Council of Churches held at Detroit during the first week in December 1969. On December fifth the Communist *Daily World* carried an article by Communist William Allen reporting that:

By unanimous vote, the 790 delegates at the convention here of the National Council of Churches condemned the massacre of Vietnamese civilians by U.S. troops.

On that same page, immediately following Comrade Allen's account, appeared a shorter item reporting yet another N.C.C. resolution recommended "that U.S. churches raise 'substantial' funds to support 60,000 American military deserters and draft resisters who have taken refuge in Canada."

The *Daily World* report also named Dr. Cynthia Wedel, "an outspoken advocate of women's rights," as having just been elected the first woman President of the National Council of Churches. The *New York Times* noted on December fifth that the new N.C.C. President now occupies the "highest symbolic post in American Protestantism." Devoting a quarter of a page to the background of Mrs. Wedel, it revealed that she maintains the position of Associate Director of the wildly Leftist Center for Voluntarism in the Institute for Applied Behavioral Science in Washington, *"the pioneering body in sensitivity training formerly known as the National Training Laboratory."* In addition, she is a leading member of the "Jeanette Rankin Brigade" — a subversive group made up largely of the wives and daughters of Communists and fellow travelers.

After receiving her doctorate in psychology from George Washington University in 1935, we are told, Mrs. Wedel "took charge of youth work for the Episcopal Church in New York." There she met and married the Reverend Theodore O. Wedel. The *Times* somehow failed to mention that the Reverend Theodore Wedel is listed in Appendix *IX* of the Dies Committee on Un-American Activities as having begun his career of support for Communist causes as early as 1940 by sponsoring a "Conference On Civil Rights" held under the auspices of a Communist Front called the Washington Committee for Democratic Action. His wife, Cynthia, was listed in the Communist *Worker* of July 14, 1957, as a signer of a Communist petition to President Eisenhower calling for a ban on H-bomb testing.

What plans have Mrs. Wedel and the leaders of the National Council for rendering further aid to the Communists? For one thing, they called on member churches at their Detroit conference to "organize the collection of funds in the churches over the Christmas season for distribution among the *Committee of Responsibility, the American Friends Service Committee, Vietnam Christian, Service and Caritas,* for emergency medical relief to civilian Vietnamese casualties....To participate in the continuation of the March Against Death in communities around the country...." In short, the N.C.C. called for the collection of money for subversive agencies have given material aid to the Communist Vietcong, and for the promotion of the Communists' continuing "Vietnam Moratorium" project.

During the course of the N.C.C.'s week-long conference, some three thousand "church leaders" were treated to the stirring words of Marxist James Forman, militant leader of the Black Nationalist movement in America. Referring to his "Black Manifesto," Forman called for "a transfer of power," asserting the hoary Communist canard about the "right of self-determination" for blacks in America.

Commenting on Forman, syndicated columnist Tom Anderson has noted:

On May 2, 1969, Marxist-anarchist James Forman presented a list of demands, called a Black Manifesto, *to the General Board of the National Council of Churches. This manifesto demands that United States churches pay 500 million dollars as "reparations" to Negroes for past "exploitation." The money would be paid to Forman's National Black Economic Development Conference to help finance a nationwide guerrilla war. The Manifesto clearly, expressed N.B.E.D.C.'s intention to overthrow the U.S. government by force and violence.*

And, believe it or not, the General Board of the N.C.C., after voting in *favor* of Foreman's plan, declared that it desired "to record its deepest appreciation to Mr. James Forman for the presentation of, and explanation concerning, the Black Manifesto...."

So you see, there is little wonder that in its issue of July 15, 1968, *Approach* magazine (a publication of the National Council of Churches) devoted considerable space to an exclusive interview with Gus Hall, General Secretary of the Communist Party, U.S.A. During that unprecedented interview, Comrade Hall declared that Communism and the church share so many goals that "they ought to exist for one another." Hall, said the N.C.C. article, "cited current red goals for America as being 'almost identical' to those espoused by the liberal church....

'We can — we should — work together for the same things," he said." You see. Communist leader Gus Hall concluded: "We can live together in a Socialist nation."

If the National Council of Churches has its way, that's *just* the way it will be!

Footnotes:

[1] The Methodist Federation for Social Service, later changed its name to become the Methodist Federation for Social Action, admitted its cooperation with the Communists in its

Bulletin number eight for 1932. It was subsequently cited as a Communist Front by the 1948 Report of the California Committee on Un-American Activities. On February 17, 1952, the House Committee on Un-American Activities Issued an 87-page document detailing the Red activities of the M.F.S.A. and its Communist personnel. Among those in this Front cited as active Communists posing as church leaders was one Winifred Chappell, a Soviet agent who was assigned by Harry Ward to do "youth work" for the Methodist Church. As Secretary of M.F.S.S. for ten years, she counseled young draftees to commit wholesale sabotage and treason against the United States. Writing in the Methodist weekly, *Epworth Herald,* Comrade Winifred advised youth to: *"Accept the draft, take the drill, go into the camps and onto the battlefield, or into the munitions factories and transportation work — but sabotage war preparations and war. Be agitators for sabotage."*

Another Communist in this outfit was the Reverend Jack McMichael, the first clergyman ever subpoenaed by the House Committee on Un-American Activities. He was Executive Secretary for the M.F.S.A. Then there was Dr. Charles C. Webber, M.F.S.S. Co-Secretary, who told an audience at Rochester Divinity School: *"Capitalism is un-Christian and unethical, and must give way, to Socialism and Communism, and the missionaries of the future must be social revolutionists."* There was also Jerome Davis, identified twice under oath as a Communist, with a record of Communist activities that takes eight full pages. The current Executive Secretary of the Methodist Federation for Social Action is Communist Lee H. Ball of Chicago.

Communist Party founder Benjamin Gitlow revealed during testimony given in 1953 that the objective of M.F.S.A. "was to transform the Methodist Church and Christianity into an instrument for the achievement of Socialism." The Communists in this organization, said Gitlow, "posed as religious reformers fighting orthodoxy and reaction in religion."

[2] Approximately one-third of those elected to the General Board of the National Council of Churches have had similar Communist records while at least seven hundred officers, denominational representatives, and other N.C.C. officials also have Communist Front records.

³ Dr. Arthur S. Flemming, currently President of the University of Oregon, served as N.C.C. President from 1966 to 1969. He was a U.S. Civil Service Commissioner in Washington during the Administration of President Franklin Roosevelt. In that strategic position, Flemming had ruled that Soviet agent Nathan Gregory Silvermaster, head of a Communist spy ring operating within our Government, was "eligible" to retain his key post. Dr. Flemming ruled favorably in behalf of a number of such Communist agents.[50]

The world Council of Churches (WCC) includes the National Council of Churches, conceives of the "kingdom of God" as a visible, social order actively promotes world socialism.

The Reverend Doctor Carl McIntire (1906-2002) an Orthodox Presbyterian fought modernism and communism and was great defender of the true Christian faith. He fought against the World Council of Churches he said consisted of 170 denominations.

The organized unorthodox church in America bears a great responsibility in our country's march into socialism. Today Christianity is being undermined by those who were never a part of the Marxist National Council of Churches. I believe that we are witnessing today the apostasy of the church. I believe most firmly in the second coming of Christ. I believe that He shall return sooner rather than later. However, I do not believe in the imminent return of Christ; that is, that He may come back at any moment. I take this position because I believe the Bible. In II Thessalonians Chapter two, the church had been falsely led to believe that Christ would return at any moment. St. Paul instructs them that two things MUST take place before the return of Christ. II Thess. 2: 3:

Let no man deceive you by any means: for that day shall not come, except there come a falling away first, and that man of sin be revealed, the son of perdition:"

---

[50] (http://www.reformed-theology.org/html/issue07/apostasy.htm)

Matthew Henry comments that the "falling away" is the general apostasy that shall precede the return of Christ. In his interpretation, Henry is in accord with the original Greek manuscript as he comments:

> By this apostasy we are not to understand a defection in the state, or from civil government, but in spiritual or religious matters, from sound doctrine, instituted worship and church government and a holy life. The apostle speaks of some very great apostasy, not only of some converted Jews or Gentiles, but such as should be very general, though gradual, and should give occasion to the revelation or rise of anti-Christ, that "man of sin."[51]

Contemporary Christian Worship and the Great Falling Away

Traditional worship services have changed very little during two millennia. I believe that the apostasy of the church is being revealed when false apostles are instilling contemporary worship services and contemporary (Christian?) music.

"For such are false apostles, deceitful workers, transforming themselves into the apostles of Christ. And no marvel; for Satan himself is transformed into an angel of light. Therefore it is no great thing if his ministers also be transformed as ministers of righteousness; whose end shall be according to their works."

A false prophet would try to conform the church to the world. Worldly means and methods would replace the old traditional form of reverence in worship. Worship must be God-centered. The

---

[51] *Matthew Henry's Commentary*, Vol. 6. 798.

people should not focus on themselves and their wants. Doing things your own way is not giving God reverence. In the Ten Commandments we are taught to put God first and are instructed in the right way to worship.

In the days of Adam and Eve it would certainly seem that there was a time, a place, and a way to worship God. Cain was not an atheist! He, as well as Abel, came to worship God. However, Cain wanted to worship God in his own way. As a result of his, God did not accept Can's sacrifice, or his worship. In jealous anger, Cain killed his own brother.

God is to be worshiped in accordance with Psalm 89:7: *"God is greatly to be feared in the assembly of the saints, and to be had in reverence of all them that are about him."*

God is to be worshiped according to Hebrews 12:28: *"Wherefore we receiving a kingdom, cannot be moved, let us have grace, whereby we may serve God acceptably with reverence and godly fear."*

You can believe that there was reverence and godly fear in the church at Jerusalem when God killed Ananias for lying. *"And great fear came upon all the church, and upon as many as heard these things."* No contemporary, slap happy worship here.

Casual dress is always stressed in the contemporary church. Blue jeans, tee shirts, shorts, anything goes in contemporary worship. If you had an audience with the Queen of England, would you show up in casual dress—certainly not! How then, can one come before the King of Kings and the Lord of Lords showing less respect than one would show to an earthly monarch?

On one of my trips to Jamaica, I worked with a missionary and preached every day in special meetings, in schools, and in open air street meetings. I looked forward to preaching at the James Hill Baptist Church on Sunday mornings. Most of the people in Jamaica are very poor. Throughout the week, most go barefoot and in ragged dress. However, on Sunday morning I watched the congregation assemble at the house of God for worship. The women wore the best dress that they had and all wore a hat. The men came in the only suit that they owned, if they had one, or at least in a white shirt with a tie. This is what is meant by showing reverence to God.

Contemporary churches like loud music with drums beating and musical instrument blaring out. Rick Warren, a Southern Baptist preacher who is unapologetically contemporary, said of his Saddleback Church, "I'll be honest with you, we are <u>loud</u>. We are really, really loud . . . We're not gonna turn it down . . ."[52] Perhaps Rick's god is sleeping and needs to be awakened.

In I Kings 18 we have the account recorded of Elijah's contest with the prophets of Baal. It was agreed that the true God would answer by fire. The prophets of Baal put on quite a show leaping around, crying aloud. Elijah began to mock them so they cried out loud, and cut themselves and put on quite a demonstration. Perhaps some of the people had to leave at this point and went home saying, "Man, didn't we have a service!" But there was no fire. Elijah prayed a short prayer of only sixty-three words (KJV) and the fire fell. Elijah did not have a LOUD service.

God did not establish the church for the entertainment of his people not to adopt worldly methods in worship. You cannot fight

---

[52] "Selecting Worship Music," *Foundation Magazine*, July 29, 2002.

a spiritual warfare with carnal weapons! II Corinthians 10:4 *"For the weapons of our warfare as not carnal...."*

God has provided what the church needs: *"And he gave some, apostles; and some prophets; and some, evangelists; and some, pastors and teachers; For the perfecting of the saints, for the work of the ministry for the edifying of the body of Christ:"* Ephesians 4:11-12.

Does the above verse of scripture mention *worship leaders* and *entertainers* that are so necessary for contemporary worship?

Of course, modern versions of the Bible translated from corrupt manuscripts are important to an apostate church. The modernistic false prophets vaccinate people with a small dose of religion to keep them from getting authentic Christianity.

Rick Warren, False Prophet

Rick Warren is a member of the one-world (CFR) Council on Foreign Relations.

Rick Warren promotes a Purpose-Driven Life rather than a Spirit – Filled life, which is consistent with his man-centered religion. He admitted through his "ministry toolbox" that the focus of his ministry has shifted from faith in God's Word to service to the world.

Rick believes that church growth strategies should be based on personal wants, not on the guidelines of God's Word. His contemporary music program is based upon a survey of what kind of music the world likes. He describes his church as "The flock that rocks." Warren, like other false prophets has reinvented God's character. The chief attribute of God, according to Warren, is love, love, love. God is presented as a God who loves Muslims, people of other religions, and also loves "gays and straights." Warren has admitted he's a big fan of lesbian activist Melissa Ethridge and has all her albums. Rick is admittedly a member of the Council on Foreign Relations.

The Holy Bible teaches that the chief attribute of God is Holiness, not love. *"Holy, holy, holy is the Lord of hosts."* Isaiah 6:3 It is said of the God of the Bible *". . . Jacob have I loved, but Esau have I hated."* Romans 9:13. And again we read *". . . thou hatest all workers of iniquity."* Psalms 5:5. This does not go along with Rick's theology. We have a Holy Father, a Holy Son, a Holy Spirit, and He has given us a Holy Bible. Furthermore God saves His elect that they should be a Holy people. Ephesians 1:4. *"According as he hath chosen us in him before the foundation of the world that we should be Holy and without blame before him in love:"* We are not chosen because we were holy by nature for we were *"by nature the children of wrath, even as others."* Ephesians 2:3. God's people are chosen because He through progressive sanctification intends to make us holy and spotless. Therefore we are to pursue after *". . . holiness, without no man shall see the Lord:"* Hebrews 12:14.

In his book, *The Purpose Driven Life,* it is apparent that Warren believes in the Carnal Christian theory and on page 297 writes, "you have a choice to make, you will be either a world-class Christian, or a worldly Christian."

According to this teaching, one can be a Christian without living for God. He will still be eternally saved but will lose his rewards.

Sin will always plague the Christian in this present life but *"... sin shall not have dominion over you."* Romans 6:14

It is also written in Romans 8: 1: *"There is therefore now no condemnation to them are in Christ Jesus, who walk not after the flesh, but after the Spirit."*

To be carnally minded is not the loss of a few rewards, but *"... to be carnally minded is death;"* Romans 8:6.

A true Christian is led by the Spirit, not driven by a purpose. We do not need a heretic's book on "the Purpose Driven Life" but we need the light of the Word of God. We must understand that God is the center, not man. A true understanding of Romans 11:36 will guide us to a correct understanding of God and the Bible. *"For of him, and through him, and to him, are all things; to whom be glory forever, Amen."*

The Purpose Driven Life of an Ex-Communist

Rick Warren has been extremely successful in selling his book, *The Purpose Driven Life*. This is a precept that may well appeal to people of any religion or no religion.

In the 1950s I attended a week of lectures at a Baptist Church by ex-communist, Kenneth Goff (1909-1972). During the years that Mr. Goff lived as an activist member of the communist party here in the U. S. A., he certainly lived a "purpose driven life." Sometimes he would live on bread and water for a week at a time so he would have more money to donate to the communist agenda. Kenneth Goff declared, "I served the Communist Party with fanatical zeal for several years. . . . My whole being was consumed with party interest. As a dedicated communist he worked for: (1)

abolition of all government, (2) abolition of inheritance, (3) abolition of family, (4) abolition of religion.

Mr. Goff spoke of the different area in which they were working to destroy our way of life. He seemed to dwell more upon the communist takeover of Hollywood among writers, producers, and directors. Hollywood is a vital nerve center for the Communist program of the United States. They hoped for a breakdown of our economic and moral structure. He named at lease forty-six communists in high places in the film industry including names like: Darryl Zanuck, Harry Warner, Sam Goldwyn, and Louis B. Mayer.

Goff left the communist party after his conversion to Christianity when he was vitally united to his Lord Jesus Christ. From then on, he lived the Spirit-led life and forever departed the "purpose driven life. This is what happens when one becomes a REAL Christian.

After several failed attempts he was finally assassinated, which typically happens to communist party defectors.

I believe that we have an example of the "purpose-driven life" in the Bible. Jonah, the prophet, received a commission from God to go to Nineveh and cry against it. Now, Nineveh was an enemy of Israel and Jonah being a patriotic Jew was afraid if he went on this mission that Nineveh *might* repent. This did not appeal to Jonah. So Jonah left the Spirit-led life and embraced the purpose-driven life directed him to get as far away from God and Nineveh as he could.

Jonah 1:3: *"But Jonah rose up to flee unto Tarshish from the presence of the Lord, and went down to Joppa; and he found a ship going to Tarshish . . . ."*

Wonderful providence! Ships did not sail everyday and certainly not to Tarshish. It looked as though God was going to bless Jonah's purpose-driven life! Almost everyone is familiar with the story of Jonah and how the purpose-driven life put him in the belly of the whale. Then in the belly of the whale, Jonah cried unto God and repented. Soon thereafter, we find Jonah in the Spirit-led life, preaching in Nineveh.

WHY SOCIALISM WILL NOT WORK

When you implement "from each according to his ability, to each according to his need," magically, everyone starts having quite a lot of need and very little ability. Ayn Rand

Marxism has always thrived on lies and deception. Karl Marx encouraged Mr. Lincoln's war because he taught that the white wage slave of the North could not be liberated until the black chattel slave of the South was liberated.

Although it may be true that laboring man has not always been treated fairly; for many, many years now, the worker in America has been well compensated.

Daniel De Leon, (1852-1914), a famous socialist leader, perpetuated one of the greatest hoaxes ever by using false calculations to show that the working man was being cheated. If true, then, the only answer to this situation would be socialism.

> On the evening of July 10, 1905, the 53 year old, tall, white-plumed, magnetic Daniel De Leon mounted the platform of the Union Temple Hall in Minneapolis to deliver an impressive address that changed the course of history and still deludes the thinking of men.
>
> De Leon began by unrolling a chart that had been prepared by the Republican National Committee for use in the Campaign of 1904. The chart showed that in 1860 manufactured products totaled a little less than $1.9 billion. The chart also showed that the workers who had produced this enormous amount of wealth were paid just under $400 million. According to De Leon, that proved

that in 1860 the working man received only $20 out of each $100 of goods produced, while the owners received $80. (Kershner, 17, 18)

According to De Leon, by 1900 the working man was receiving only $17 for each $100 worth of goods he produced. This report quickly spread around the world and for a while went unchallenged.

In 1936 the U. S. government did a complete survey of every line of industry in the country. It showed that employees actually received 85% and the owners 15% of each $100 worth of goods produced. The U. S. Department of Commerce concluded that their survey that the working man received 87.5 cents from every dollar of goods produced.

What about the compensation for the slave in the Antebellum South? According to economists and social scientists, Fogel and Engerman, "over the course of his lifetime, the typical slave field-hand received about 90% of the income he produced (*Antebellum Slavery*, 32)."

Fitting Quotes by Thomas Jefferson for Our Time

After his brief fascination with French Enlightenment philosophies, which occurred around 1776, Thomas Jefferson left us a legacy of insightful comments on government.

> The God who gave us life, gave us liberty at the same time.

> The democracy will cease to exist when you take away from those who are willing to work and give to those who would not.

It is incumbent on every generation to pay its own debts as it goes. A principle if acted on would save one-half the wars of the world.

I predict future happiness for Americans if they can prevent the government from wasting the labors of the people under the pretense of taking care of them.

My reading of history convinces me that most bad government results from too much government.

No free man shall ever be debarred the use of arms. The strongest reason for the people to retain the right to keep and bear arms is, as a last resort, to protect themselves against tyranny in government.

The tree of liberty must be refreshed from time to time with the blood of patriots and tyrants.

To compel a man to subsidize with his taxes the propagation of ideas that he disbelieves and abhors is sinful and tyrannical.

Paper is poverty,... it is only the ghost of money, and not money itself.

>Letter to Colonel Edward Carrington (27 May 1788)

I consider the foundation of the Constitution as laid on this ground: That "all powers not delegated to the United States, by the Constitution, nor prohibited by it to the States, are reserved to the States or to the people."

I agree with you that there is a natural aristocracy among men. The grounds of this are virtue and talents. Letter to John Adams (28 October 1813).

"The trouble with socialism is that you eventually run out of other people's money." ~ *Margaret Thatcher*

You cannot legislate the poor into freedom by legislating the industrious out of it. You don't multiply wealth by dividing it. Government cannot give anything to anybody that it doesn't first take from somebody else. Whenever somebody receives something without working for it, somebody else has to work for it without receiving. The worst thing that can happen to a nation is for half of the people to get the idea they don't have to work because somebody else will work for them, and the other half to get the idea that it does no good to work because they don't get to enjoy the fruit of their labor.[53]

Let's suppose that a group of ten graduate students regularly go out to a pub for beer, and the tab for the ten comes to $100 total. If they pay for their bill the way Americans pay for our taxes (based on our so-called "progressive" tax system), the breakout would be like this: The first four people (the poorest) pay nothing. They get to drink for free. The fifth pays $1. The sixth pays $3. The seventh pays $7. The eighth pays $12. The ninth pays $18. The tenth person (the richest) pays $59. Being good friends and liberal progressives, that's what they all agree to do. It seems only fair that each person should pay what they can afford to pay, remembering the old adage they learned in school: "from each according to his ability, to each according to his need." (Karl Marx). Every few days, the 10 good friends would meet up in the pub and would pay up as agreed upon. Then one day, the proprietor gave them a deal. "Since you are such good customers, from now on", he said, "I'm going to reduce the cost of your tab by $20. You can just pay

---

[53] Rogers, Adrian, *Ten Secrets for a Successful Family,* 138.

me $80!" Everyone wanted to continue to pay their bill just the same way as they had before. So the first four people (the poorest) are unaffected. They continue to get to drink for free. But what about the remaining 6 people? How should they split up the unexpected $20 savings "windfall" so that everyone would get "his fair share"? They figured that $20 shared by 6 comes out to $3.33 each. But if they simply subtracted that amount from each of the 6 paying friends, then person #5 and person #6 would actually be paid to have their beers since person #5 only paid $1 anyway and person #6 only paid $3! What to do? The pub owner came to their rescue. He suggested that each person's bill should be reduced by roughly the same amount, and he used his calculator to work out what that should be: Persons 1-4 continue to get to drink for free. The fifth person, like the first four, now pays nothing and drinks for free (100% savings!). The sixth pays just $2 instead of the original $3 (33% savings!). The seventh pays just $5 instead of the original $7 (28% savings!). The eighth pays just $9 instead of the original $12 (25% savings!). The ninth pays just $15 instead of the original $18 (17% savings!). The tenth pays just $49 instead of the original $59 (16% savings!). All 6 friends were better off than before. And their first four buddies continued to drink for free, because they didn't have a lot of money. They all felt pretty good about it. After they thanked the pub owner and left to walk back to campus, they began to compare their savings under this new deal. The sixth person was very quiet, though. Finally he blurted out. "You know, splitting up the bill that way wasn't fair! I only got a dollar out of that $20 we all saved, and yet (he pointed to the tenth person) he got $10!" "Hey, you're right", shouted the seventh person. "I got cheated too. I only saved 2 dollars. It's unfair that he got back 5 times more than me!" "Damn it! I've been ripped off too", yelled the eighth. "Why should he get back $10 when I got back only $3. The wealthy get all the breaks!" "Wait a minute", screamed friends one through four. "We didn't get anything at all! The system exploits the poor!" The first nine people surrounded the tenth person and beat him up. The next day, tempers had cooled down and the nine friends showed back up at the pub. They were sorry for what they had done and they wanted to apologize to their tenth friend. But the tenth person didn't show up for drinks. So the nine proceeded to drink without him. When it came time to pay the tab, they discovered that they had a problem. They didn't have enough money among all nine of them to pay for even half of the bill! "And that, boys and girls, journalists and college professors, is how our tax system works", says Professor Kamershen. "The people who pay the highest taxes get the most benefit from a tax reduction. Tax them too much, attack them for being wealthy, and they just may not show up anymore. In fact, they might start drinking overseas where the atmosphere is somewhat friendlier." President Obama and the Democratically-controlled congress, good wannabe socialists all, should remember this lessen before all of the rich people (mostly Democrats, by the way, but that's the topic of another article) stop going to the pub with all their other good friends. Raising taxes using a "progressive" tax system penalizes the productive, wealthiest members of our society much more than the average taxpayer. And I'm against that even though it would hurt the many Democrat billionaires far more. And once we tip over the edge where 50% of the population don't pay income tax at all (the first five "good friends"), we create an "us-

and-them" mentality where the first five vote in the politicians they want to continue to get their beers for free. But there's no such thing as a free lunch. Someone always pays. Until they can't or don't anymore. John Galt couldn't have said it plainer.(Terry Easton, "How Socialism Works in the Real World" May 14, 2009; http://www.humanevents.com/article.php?id=31861)

And a final illustration of how socialism doesn't work:

An economics professor at Texas Tech said he had never failed a single student before but had, once, failed an entire class. That class had insisted that socialism worked and that no one would be poor and no one would be rich, a great equalizer. The professor then said okay, we will have an experiment in this class on socialism. All grades would be averaged and everyone would receive the same grade, so no one would fail and no one would receive an 'A'. After the first test the grades were averaged and everyone got a 'B'. The students who studied hard were upset and the students who studied little were happy. But, as the second test rolled around, the students who studied little had studied even less and the ones who studied hard decided they wanted a free ride too; so they studied little. The second test average was a 'D'! No one was happy. When the 3rd test rolled around the average was an 'F'. The scores never increased as bickering, blame, name-calling all resulted in hard feelings and no one would study for the benefit of anyone else. All failed, to their great surprise, and the professor told them that socialism would also ultimately fail because when the reward is great, the effort to succeed is great; But when government takes all the reward away; no one will try or want to succeed.
(http://www.scribd.com/doc/16965280/Why-Socialism-Doesnt-Work)

GLOBAL WARMING AND THE SOCIALIST AGENDA

The section on the deception of "Global Warming" is clearly an attempt to gain control over our lives. Several years ago the government took over control of our toilets, now they want to control our thermostats.

It is ridiculous to suppose that puny man can *ever* control the climate of our earth. Natural disasters are under control of God. They may and can change our climate but *man* has not will never progress into becoming as powerful as God.

Excerpts from the following three editorials should be convincing enough to persuade a rational human being that global warming is a hoax:

> It's Time for a Global Warming Update
>
> Walter Williams
>
> John Coleman, founder of the Weather Channel, in an hour-long television documentary titled "Global Warming: The Other Side."
>
> . . .During the 1960s and into the 1980s, the number of stations used for calculating global surface temperatures was about 6,000. By 1990, the number of stations dropped rapidly to about 1,500. Most of the stations lost were in the colder regions of the Earth. Not adjusting for their lost made temperatures appear to be higher than was in fact the case. According to Science & Environmental Policy Project, Russia reported that CRU was ignoring data from colder regions of Russia, even though these stations were still reporting data. That

means data loss was not simply the result of station closings but deliberate decisions by CRU to ignore them in order to hype their global warming claims. D'Aleo and Smith report that our NCDC engaged in similar deceptive activity where they have dropped stations, particularly in colder climates, higher elevations or closer to the polar regions. Temperatures are now simply projected for these colder stations from other stations, usually in warmer climates.

Mounting evidence of scientific fraud might make little difference in terms of the response to manmade global warming hysteria. Why? Vested economic and political interests have emerged where trillions of dollars and social control are at stake. Therefore, many people who recognize the scientific fraud underlying global warming claims are likely to defend it anyway. Automobile companies have invested billions in research and investment in producing "green cars." General Electric and Phillips have spent millions lobbying Congress to outlaw incandescent bulbs so that they can force us to buy costly compact fluorescent light bulbs (CFL). Farmers and ethanol manufacturers have gotten Congress to enact laws mandating greater use of their product, not to mention massive subsidies. Thousands of major corporations around the world have taken steps to reduce carbon emissions including giants like IBM, Nike, Coca-Cola and BP, the oil giant. Companies like Google, Yahoo and Dell have vowed to become "carbon neutral." Then there's Chicago Climate Futures Exchange that plans to trade in billions of dollars of greenhouse gas emission allowances. Corporate America and labor unions, as well as their international counterparts have a huge multi-trillion dollar financial stake in the perpetuation of the global warming fraud. Federal, state and local agencies have spent billions of dollars and created millions of jobs to deal with one aspect or another of global warming.

It's deeper than just money. Schoolteachers have created polar-bear-dying lectures to frighten and indoctrinate our children when in fact there are more polar bears now than in 1950. They've taught children about melting glaciers. Just recently, the International Panel on Climate Change was forced to admit that their Himalayan glacier-melting fraud was done to "impact policy makers and politicians and encourage them to take some concrete action."

What would all the beneficiaries of the global warming hype do if it becomes widely known and accepted that mankind's activities have very little to do with the Earth's temperature? I don't know, but a lot of people would feel and look like idiots. But I bet that even if the permafrost returned as far south as New Jersey, as it once did, the warmers and their congressional stooges would still call for measures to fight global warming.

Obama Climate Czar Has Socialist Ties

Stephen Dinan

January 12, 2009

Until last week, Carol M. Browner, President-elect Barack Obama's pick as global warming czar, was listed as one of 14 leaders of a socialist group's Commission for a Sustainable World Society, which calls for "global governance" and says rich countries must shrink their economies to address climate change.

By Thursday, Mrs. Browner's name and biography had been removed from Socialist International's Web page, though a photo of her speaking June 30 to the group's congress in Greece was still available.

Socialist International, an umbrella group for many of the world's social democratic political parties such as Britain's Labor Party, says it supports socialism and is harshly critical of U.S. policies.

The group's Commission for a Sustainable World Society, the organization's action arm on climate change, says the developed world must reduce consumption and commit to binding and punitive limits on greenhouse gas emissions.

Mr. Obama, who has said action on climate change would be a priority in his administration, tapped Mrs. Browner last month to fill a new position as White House coordinator of climate and energy policies. The appointment does not need Senate confirmation.

Mr. Obama's transition team said Mrs. Browner's membership in the organization is not a problem and that it brings experience in U.S. policymaking to her new role.

"The Commission for a Sustainable World Society includes world leaders from a variety of political parties, including British Prime Minister Gordon Brown, who succeeded Tony Blair, in serving as vice president of the convening organization," Obama transition spokesman Nick Shapiro said.

"Carol Browner was chosen to help the president-elect coordinate energy and climate policy because she understands that our efforts to create jobs, achieve energy security and combat climate change demand integration among different agencies; cooperation between federal, state and local governments; and partnership with the private sector," Mr. Shapiro said in an e-mail.

Mrs. Browner ran the Environmental Protection Agency under President Clinton. Until she was tapped for the Obama administration, she was on the board of directors for the National Audubon Society, the League of Conservation Voters, the Center for American Progress and former Vice President Al Gore's Alliance for Climate Protection.

Her name has been removed from the Gore organization's Web site list of directors, and the Audubon Society issued a press release about her departure from that organization.

Republicans said Mrs. Browner's work with Socialist International raises questions.

"Does she agree with the group's positions on global governance – that the United States should abdicate its international leadership to international organizations? Does she support its position that the international community should be the ultimate arbiter of climate change policy?" said Antonia Ferrier, a spokeswoman for House Minority Leader John A. Boehner, Ohio Republican.

"These are questions that merit answers – especially when you consider this group's deep skepticism about America's ability to be a force for positive change in the world," she said.

An aide on the Obama team said its information shows that Mrs. Browner resigned from the organization in June 2008. The aide, who asked not to be named because he was discussing internal matters, said the transition team was aware she had been a member of the group when she was vetted.

The Socialist International Web site didn't have a copy of her June 30 speech, but the agenda for the meeting had her scheduled to speak as part of a panel on "How do we strengthen the multilateral architecture for a sustainable future?"

Other panel participants were Sergey Mironov, speaker of the Russian legislature's upper chamber and a close ally of Prime Minister Vladimir Putin; Zhang Zhijun, vice minister of the International Department of the Chinese Communist Party's Central Committee; and Jesus Caldera, a former Minister of Employment and Social Affairs of the Spanish Socialist Workers' Party.

A woman answering the phone at Socialist International's headquarters in London said all officers were traveling.

Nobody from the organization returned a message left Friday.

Socialist International bills itself as the world body of democratic socialist movements. It includes members ranging from Israel's Labor Party and France's Socialist Party to Angola's MPLA, which won the 1970s Angolan civil war with the aid of Soviet arms and Cuban troops.

The organization distinguishes itself from violent or revolutionary communist parties. However, some such groups, including the Chinese Communist Party, have been invited to its events as guest organizations.

The Democratic Socialists of America, not the Democratic Party, is listed as the group's U.S. representative. But Mrs. Browner was listed as an individual member of Socialist International, but not a member of the DSA.

While agreeing with Mr. Obama on the need for action to address climate change, the organization wants more draconian policies than the president-elect's preferred solution.

During the presidential campaign, Mr. Obama called for a cap-and-trade system to control carbon emissions. He argued that such a system is efficient and lets the free market determine where it's easiest to reduce greenhouse gas emissions.

Socialist International says such "flexible mechanisms" do not clamp down hard enough on polluters.

The organization often takes a decidedly critical view of the U.S.

At this summer's meeting, the group issued a statement on economics that blasted the "neo-liberal market ideology and the unilateralist, U.S.-dominated approach in the global economic system," and attacked the U.S. for dominating international financial institutions.

At its meeting earlier in 2008 in Santiago, Chile, Socialist International endorsed "global governance" as the solution to the world's problems of peace and climate change.

At a July meeting in St. Petersburg, the commission said developed countries "should think of decreasing current consumption levels" – would mean shrinking their economies – in order to help the environment.

Socialist International regularly blasts the construction of fencing along the U.S.-Mexico border. The fence was approved by both houses of Congress, including with Mr. Obama's vote in the Senate.

Socialist International was congratulatory when Mr. Obama won the election, issuing a statement noting that "the sky may seem a bit brighter today" but warning still that "there are enormous global challenges that must be addressed effectively and without delay.

(http://globalwarminghoax.wordpress.com/2009/01/12/obama-climate-czar-has-socialist-ties/)

2008 Was the Year Man-Made Global Warming Was Disproved

Christopher Booker, British Journalist

December 27, 2008

London *Telegraph*

Easily one of the most important stories of 2008 has been all the evidence suggesting that this may be looked back on as the year when there was a turning point in the great worldwide panic over man-made global warming. Just when politicians in Europe and America have been adopting the most costly and damaging measures politicians have ever proposed, to combat this supposed menace, the tide has turned in three significant respects.

First, all over the world, temperatures have been dropping in a way wholly unpredicted by all those computer models have been used as the main drivers of the scare. Last winter, as temperatures plummeted, many parts of the world had snowfalls on a scale not seen for decades. This winter, with the whole of Canada and half the US under snow, looks likely to be even worse. After several years flat-lining, global temperatures have dropped sharply enough to cancel out much of their net rise in the 20th century.

Ever shriller and more frantic has become the insistence of the warmists, cheered on by their army of media groupies such as the BBC, that the last 10 years have been the "hottest in history" and that the North Pole would soon be ice-free – as the poles remain defiantly icebound and those polar bears fail to drown. All those hysterical predictions that we are seeing more droughts and hurricanes than ever before have infuriatingly failed to materialise.

Even the more cautious scientific acolytes of the official orthodoxy now admit that, thanks to "natural factors" such as ocean currents, temperatures have failed to rise as predicted (although they plaintively assure us that this cooling effect is merely "masking the underlying warming trend", and that the temperature rise will resume worse than ever by the middle of the next decade).

Secondly, 2008 was the year when any pretence that there was a "scientific consensus" in favour of man-made global warming collapsed. At long last, as in the Manhattan Declaration last March, hundreds of proper scientists, including many of the world's most eminent climate experts, have been rallying to pour scorn on that "consensus" was only a politically engineered artifact, based on ever more blatantly manipulated data and computer models programmed to produce no more than convenient fictions.

Thirdly, as banks collapsed and the global economy plunged into its worst recession for decades, harsh reality at last began to break in on those self-deluding dreams have for so long possessed almost every politician in the western world. As we saw in this month's Poznan conference, when 10,000 politicians, officials and "environmentalists" gathered to plan next year's "son of Kyoto" treaty in Copenhagen, panicking politicians are waking up to the fact that the world can no longer afford all those quixotic schemes for "combating climate change" with they were so happy to indulge themselves in more comfortable times.

Suddenly it has become rather less appealing that we should divert trillions of dollars, pounds and euros into the fantasy that we could reduce emissions of carbon dioxide by 80 per cent. All those grandiose projects for "emissions trading", "carbon capture", building tens of thousands more useless wind turbines, switching vast areas of farmland from producing food to "bio-fuels", are being exposed as no more than enormously damaging and futile gestures, costing astronomic sums we no longer possess.

As 2009 dawns, it is time we in Britain faced up to the genuine crisis now fast approaching from the fact that – unless we get on very soon with building enough proper power stations to fill our looming "energy gap" - within a few years our lights will go out and what remains of our economy will judder to a halt. After years of infantile displacement activity, it is high time our politicians – along with those of the EU and President Obama's US – were brought back with a mighty jolt into contact with the real world.

(http://www.telegraph.co.uk/comment/columnists/christopherbooker/3982101/2008-was-the-year-man-made-global-warming-was-disproved.html)

Senate Environment and Public Works Committee Report

Friday December 21, 2007

INTRODUCTION:

Over 400 prominent scientists from more than two dozen countries recently voiced significant objections to major aspects of the so-called "consensus" on man-made global warming. These scientists, many of whom are current and former participants in the UN IPCC (Intergovernmental Panel on Climate Change), criticized the climate claims made by the UN IPCC and former Vice President Al Gore. The new report issued by the Senate Environment and Public Works Committee's office of the GOP Ranking Member details the views of the scientists, the overwhelming majority of whom spoke out in 2007.

Even some in the establishment media now appear to be taking notice of the growing number of skeptical scientists. In October, the Washington Post Staff Writer Juliet Eilperin conceded the obvious, writing that climate skeptics "appear to be expanding rather than shrinking." Many scientists from around the world have dubbed 2007 as the year man-made global warming fears "bite the dust." In addition, many scientists who are also progressive environmentalists believe climate fear promotion has "co-opted" the green movement.

This blockbuster Senate report lists the scientists by name, country of residence, and academic/institutional affiliation. It also features their own words, biographies, and web-links to their peer reviewed studies and original source materials as gathered from public statements, various news outlets, and websites in 2007. This new "consensus busters" report is poised to redefine the debate.

Many of the scientists featured in this report consistently stated that numerous colleagues shared their views, but they will not speak out publicly for fear of retribution. Atmospheric scientist Dr. Nathan Paldor, Professor of Dynamical Meteorology and Physical Oceanography at the Hebrew University of Jerusalem, author of almost 70 peer-reviewed studies, explains how many of his fellow scientists have been intimidated.

"Many of my colleagues with whom I spoke share these views and report on their inability to publish their skepticism in the scientific or public media," Paldor wrote. Scientists from Around the World Dissent This new report details how teams of international scientists are dissenting from the UN IPCC's view of climate science. In such nations as Germany, Brazil, the Netherlands, Russia, New Zealand and France, nations, scientists banded together in 2007 to oppose climate alarmism. In addition, over 100 prominent international scientists sent an open letter in December 2007 to the UN stating attempts to control climate were "futile." Paleo-climatologist Dr. Tim Patterson, professor in the department of Earth Sciences at Carleton University in Ottawa, recently converted from a believer in man-made climate change to a skeptic. Patterson noted that the notion of a "consensus" of scientists aligned with the UN IPCC or former Vice President Al Gore is false. "I was at the Geological Society of America meeting in Philadelphia in the fall and I would say that people with my opinion were probably in the majority."

This new committee report, a first of its kind, comes after the UN IPCC chairman Rajendra Pachauri implied that there were only "about a dozen" skeptical scientists left in the world. Former Vice President Gore has claimed that scientists skeptical of climate change are akin to "flat Earth society members" and similar in number to those who "believe the moon landing was actually staged in a movie lot in Arizona."

The distinguished scientists featured in this new report are experts in diverse fields, including: climatology; oceanography; geology; biology; glaciology; biogeography; meteorology; oceanography; economics; chemistry; mathematics; environmental sciences; engineering; physics and paleo-climatology. Some of those profiled have won Nobel Prizes for their outstanding contribution to their field of expertise and many shared a portion of the UN IPCC Nobel Peace Prize with Vice President Gore. Additionally, these scientists hail from prestigious institutions worldwide, including: Harvard University; NASA; National Oceanic and Atmospheric Administration (NOAA) and the National Center for Atmospheric Research (NCAR); Massachusetts Institute of Technology; the UN IPCC; the Danish National Space Center; U.S. Department of Energy; Princeton University; the Environmental Protection Agency; University of Pennsylvania; Hebrew University of Jerusalem; the International Arctic Research Centre; the Pasteur Institute in Paris; the Belgian Weather Institute; Royal Netherlands Meteorological Institute; the University of Helsinki; the National Academy of Sciences of the U.S., France, and Russia; the University of Pretoria; University of Notre Dame; Stockholm University; University of Melbourne; Columbia University; the World Federation of

Scientists; and the University of London. The voices of many of these hundreds of scientists serve as a direct challenge to the often media-hyped "consensus" that the debate is "settled." A May 2007 Senate report detailed scientists who had recently converted from believers in man-made global warming to skepticism. [See May 15, 2007 report: Climate Momentum Shifting: Prominent Scientists Reverse Belief in Man-made Global Warming - Now Skeptics: Growing Number of Scientists Convert to Skeptics After Reviewing New Research – In addition, an August 2007 report detailed how proponents of man-made global warming fears enjoy a monumental funding advantage over skeptical scientists.] This report counters the claims made by the promoters of man-made global warming fears that the number of skeptical scientists is dwindling. Examples of "consensus" claims made by promoters of man-made climate fears: Former Vice President Al Gore (November 5, 2007): "There are still people who believe that the Earth is flat." Gore also compared global warming skeptics to people who 'believe the moon landing was actually staged in a movie lot in Arizona' (June 20, 2006) CNN's Miles O'Brien (July 23, 2007): The scientific debate is over." "We're done." O'Brien also declared on CNN on February 9, 2006 that scientific skeptics of man-made catastrophic global warming "are bought and paid for by the fossil fuel industry, usually."

On July 27, 2006, Associated Press reporter Seth Borenstein described a scientist as "one of the few remaining scientists skeptical of the global warming harm caused by industries that burn fossil fuels." Dr. Rajendra Pachauri, Chairman of the IPCC view on the number of skeptical scientists as quoted on Feb. 20, 2003: "About 300 years ago, a Flat Earth Society was founded by those who did not believe the world was round. That society still exists; it probably has about a dozen members."Agence France-Press (AFP Press) article (December 4, 2007): The article noted that a prominent skeptic "finds himself increasingly alone in his claim that climate change poses no imminent threat to the planet." Andrew Dessler in the eco-publication Grist Magazine (November 21, 2007): "While some people claim there are lots of skeptical climate scientists out there, if you actually try to find one, you keep turning up the same two dozen or so (e.g., Singer, Lindzen, Michaels, Christy, etc., etc.). These skeptics are endlessly recycled by the denial machine, so someone not paying close attention might think there are lots of them out there -- but that's not the case. The Washington Post asserted on May 23, 2006 that there were only "a handful of skeptics" of man-made climate fears. UN special climate envoy Dr. Gro Harlem Brundtland on May 10, 2007 declared the climate debate "over" and added "it's completely immoral, even, to question" the UN's scientific "consensus." ABC News Global Warming Reporter Bill Blakemore reported on August 30, 2006: "After extensive searches, ABC News has found no such [scientific] debate" on global warming.

Brief highlights of the report featuring over 400 international scientists:

Israel: Dr. Nathan Paldor, Professor of Dynamical Meteorology and Physical Oceanography at the Hebrew University of Jerusalem has authored almost 70 peer-reviewed studies and won several awards. "First, temperature changes, as well as rates of temperature changes (both increase and decrease) of magnitudes similar to that reported by IPCC to have occurred since the Industrial revolution (about 0.8C in 150 years or even 0.4C in the last 35 years) have occurred in Earth's climatic history. There's nothing special about the recent rise!"

Russia: Russian scientist Dr. Oleg Sorochtin of the Institute of Oceanology at the Russian Academy of Sciences has authored more than 300 studies, nine books, and a 2006 paper titled "The Evolution and the Prediction of Global Climate Changes on Earth." "Even if the concentration of 'greenhouse gases' double man would not perceive the temperature impact," Sorochtin wrote.

Spain: Anton Uriarte, a professor of Physical Geography at the University of the Basque Country in Spain and author of a book on the paleo-climate, rejected man-made climate fears in 2007. "There's no need to be worried. It's very interesting to study [climate change], but there's no need to be worried," Uriate wrote.

Netherlands: Atmospheric scientist Dr. Hendrik Tennekes, a scientific pioneer in the development of numerical weather prediction and former director of research at The Netherlands' Royal National Meteorological Institute, and an internationally recognized expert in atmospheric boundary layer processes, "I find the Doomsday picture Al Gore is painting – a six-meter sea level rise, fifteen times the IPCC number – entirely without merit," Tennekes wrote. "I protest vigorously the idea that the climate reacts like a home heating system to a changed setting of the thermostat: just turn the dial, and the desired temperature will soon be reached."

Brazil: Chief Meteorologist Eugenio Hackbart of the MetSul Meteorologia Weather Center in Sao Leopoldo – Rio Grande do Sul, Brazil declared himself a skeptic. "The media is promoting an unprecedented hyping related to global warming. The media and many scientists are ignoring very important facts that point to a natural variation in the climate system as the cause of the recent global warming," Hackbart wrote on May 30, 2007.

France: Climatologist Dr. Marcel Leroux, former professor at Université Jean Moulin and director of the Laboratory of Climatology, Risks, and Environment in Lyon, is a climate skeptic. Leroux wrote a 2005 book titled Global Warming – Myth or Reality? - The Erring Ways of Climatology. "Day after day, the same mantra - that 'the Earth is warming up' - is churned out in all its forms. As 'the ice melts' and 'sea level rises,' the Apocalypse looms ever nearer! Without realizing it, or perhaps without wishing to, the average citizen in bamboozled, lobotomized, lulled into mindless acceptance. ... Non-believers in the greenhouse scenario are in the position of those long ago who doubted the existence of God ... fortunately for them, the Inquisition is no longer with us!"

Norway: Geologist/Geochemist Dr. Tom V. Segalstad, a professor and head of the Geological Museum at the University of Oslo and formerly an expert reviewer with the UN IPCC: "It is a search for a mythical CO_2 sink to explain an immeasurable CO_2 lifetime to fit a hypothetical CO_2 computer model that purports to show that an impossible amount of fossil fuel burning is heating the atmosphere. It is all a fiction."

Finland: Dr. Boris Winterhalter, retired Senior Marine Researcher of the Geological Survey of Finland and former professor of marine geology at University of Helsinki, criticized the media for what he considered its alarming climate coverage. "The effect of solar winds on cosmic radiation has just recently been established and, furthermore, there seems to be a good correlation between cloudiness and variations in the intensity of cosmic radiation. Here we have a mechanism is a far better explanation to variations in global climate than the attempts by IPCC to blame it all on anthropogenic input of greenhouse gases. "

Germany: Paleo-climate expert Augusto Mangini of the University of Heidelberg in Germany, criticized the UN IPCC summary. "I consider the part of the IPCC report, I can really judge as an expert, i.e. the reconstruction of the paleo-climate, wrong," Mangini noted in an April 5, 2007 article. He added: "The earth will not die."

Canada: IPCC 2007 Expert Reviewer Madhav Khandekar, a PhD meteorologist, a scientist with the Natural Resources Stewardship Project who has over 45 years experience in climatology, meteorology and oceanography, and who has published nearly 100 papers, reports, book reviews and a book on Ocean Wave Analysis and Modeling: "To my dismay, IPCC authors ignored all my comments and suggestions for major changes in the FOD (First Order Draft) and sent me the SOD (Second Order Draft) with essentially the same text as the FOD. None of the authors of the chapter bothered to directly communicate with me (or with other expert reviewers with whom I communicate on a regular basis) on many issues that were raised in my review. This is not an acceptable scientific review process."

Czech Republic: Czech-born U.S. climatologist Dr. George Kukla, a research scientist with the Lamont-Doherty Earth Observatory at Columbia University, expressed climate skepticism in 2007. "The only thing to worry about is the damage that can be done by worrying. Why are some scientists worried? Perhaps because they feel that to stop worrying may mean to stop being paid," Kukla told Gelf Magazine on April 24, 2007.

India: One of India's leading geologists, B.P. Radhakrishna, President of the Geological Society of India, expressed climate skepticism in 2007. "We appear to be overplaying this global warming issue as global warming is nothing new. It has happened in the past, not once but several times, giving rise to glacial-interglacial cycles."

USA: Climatologist Robert Durenberger, past president of the American Association of State Climatologists, and one of the climatologists who gathered at Woods Hole to review the National Climate Program Plan in July, 1979: "Al Gore brought me back to the battle and prompted me to do renewed research in the field of climatology. And because of all the misinformation that Gore and his army have been spreading about climate change I have decided that 'real' climatologists should try to help the public understand the nature of the problem."

Italy: Internationally renowned scientist Dr. Antonio Zichichi, president of the World Federation of Scientists and a retired Professor of Advanced Physics at the University of Bologna in Italy, who has published over 800 scientific papers: "Significant new peer-reviewed research has cast even more doubt on the hypothesis of dangerous human-caused global warming."

New Zealand: IPCC reviewer and climate researcher Dr. Vincent Gray, an expert reviewer on every single draft of the IPCC reports going back to 1990 and author of The Greenhouse Delusion: A Critique of "Climate Change 2001: "The [IPCC] 'Summary for Policymakers' might get a few readers, but the main purpose of the report is to provide a spurious scientific backup for the absurd claims of the worldwide environmentalist lobby that it has been established scientifically that increases in carbon dioxide are harmful to the climate. It just does not matter that this ain't so."

South Africa: Dr. Kelvin Kemm, formerly a scientist at South Africa's Atomic Energy Corporation who holds degrees in nuclear physics and mathematics: "The global-warming mania continues with more and more hype and less and less thinking. With religious zeal, people look for issues or events to blame on global warming."

Poland: Physicist Dr. Zbigniew Jaworowski, Chairman of the Central Laboratory for the United Nations Scientific Committee on the Effects of Radiological Protection in Warsaw: ""We thus find ourselves in the situation that the entire theory of man-made global warming—with its repercussions in science, and its important consequences for politics and the global economy—is based on ice core studies that provided a false picture of the atmospheric CO2 levels."

Australia: Prize-winning Geologist Dr. Ian Plimer, a professor of Earth and Environmental Sciences at the University of Adelaide in Australia: "There is new work emerging even in the last few weeks that shows we can have a very close correlation between the temperatures of the Earth and supernova and solar radiation."

Britain: Dr. Richard Courtney, a UN IPCC expert reviewer and a UK-based climate and atmospheric science consultant: "To date, no convincing evidence for AGW (anthropogenic global warming) has been discovered. And recent global climate behavior is not consistent with AGW model predictions."

China: Chinese Scientists Say C02 Impact on Warming May Be 'Excessively Exaggerated' – Scientists Lin Zhen-Shan's and Sun Xian's 2007 study published in the peer-reviewed journal Meteorology and Atmospheric Physics: "Although the CO2 greenhouse effect on global climate change is unsuspicious, it could have been excessively exaggerated." Their study asserted that "it is high time to reconsider the trend of global climate change."

Denmark: Space physicist Dr. Eigil Friis-Christensen is the director of the Danish National Space Centre, a member of the space research advisory committee of the Swedish National Space Board, a member of a NASA working group, and a member of the European Space Agency who has authored or co-authored around 100 peer-reviewed papers and chairs the Institute of Space Physics: **"The <u>sun</u> is the source of the energy that causes the motion of the atmosphere and thereby controls weather and climate.** Any change in the energy from the sun received at the Earth's surface will therefore affect climate."

Belgium: Climate scientist Luc Debontridder of the Belgium Weather Institute's Royal Meteorological Institute (RMI) co-authored a study in August 2007 dismissed a decisive role of CO2 in global warming: "CO2 is not the big bogeyman of climate change and global warming. "Not CO2, but water vapor is the most important greenhouse gas. It is responsible for at least 75 % of the greenhouse effect. This is a simple scientific fact, but Al Gore's movie has hyped CO2 so much that nobody seems to take note of it."

Sweden: Geologist Dr. Wibjorn Karlen, professor emeritus of the Department of Physical Geography and Quaternary Geology at Stockholm University, critiqued the Associated Press for hyping promoting climate fears in 2007. "Another of these hysterical views of our climate. Newspapers should think about the damage they are doing to many persons, particularly young kids, by spreading the exaggerated views of a human impact on climate."

USA: Dr. David Wojick is a UN IPCC expert reviewer, who earned his PhD in Philosophy of Science and co-founded the Department of Engineering and Public Policy at Carnegie-Mellon University: "In point of fact, the hypothesis that solar variability and not human activity is warming the oceans goes a long way to explain the puzzling idea that the Earth's surface may be warming while the atmosphere is not. The GHG (greenhouse gas) hypothesis does not do this." Wojick added: "The public is not well served by this constant drumbeat of false alarms fed by computer models manipulated by advocates."

Background: Only 52 Scientists Participated in UN IPCC Summary. The over 400 skeptical scientists featured in this new report outnumber by nearly eight times the number of scientists who participated in the

2007 UN IPCC Summary for Policymakers. The notion of "hundreds" or "thousands" of UN scientists agreeing to a scientific statement does not hold up to scrutiny. (See report debunking "consensus") Recent research by Australian climate data analyst Dr. John McLean revealed that the IPCC's peer-review process for the Summary for Policymakers leaves much to be desired.

Proponents of man-made global warming like to note how the National Academy of Sciences (NAS) and the American Meteorological Society (AMS) have issued statements endorsing the so-called "consensus" view that man is driving global warming. But both the NAS and AMS never allowed member scientists to directly vote on these climate statements. Essentially, only two dozen or so members on the governing boards of these institutions produced the "consensus" statements. This report gives a voice to the rank-and-file scientists who were shut out of the process.

The most recent attempt to imply there was an overwhelming scientific "consensus" in favor of man-made global warming fears came in December 2007 during the UN climate conference in Bali. A letter signed by only 215 scientists urged the UN to mandate deep cuts in carbon dioxide emissions by 2050. But absent from the letter were the signatures of these alleged "thousands" of scientists. (See AP article:

UN IPCC chairman Rajendra Pachauri urged the world at the December 2007 UN climate conference in Bali, Indonesia to "Please listen to the voice of science.")

The science has continued to grow loud and clear in 2007. In addition to the growing number of scientists expressing skepticism, an abundance of recent peer-reviewed studies have cast considerable doubt about man-made global warming fears. A November 3, 2007 peer-reviewed study found that "solar changes significantly alter climate." A December 2007 peer-reviewed study recalculated and halved the global average surface temperature trend between 1980 – 2002. Another new study found the Medieval Warm Period "0.3C warmer than 20th century"

A peer-reviewed study by a team of scientists found that "warming is naturally caused and shows no human influence." – Another November 2007 peer-reviewed study in the journal Physical Geography found "Long-term climate change is driven by solar insulation changes." These recent studies were in addition to the abundance of peer-reviewed studies earlier in 2007. - See "New Peer-Reviewed Scientific Studies Chill Global Warming Fears." With this new report of profiling 400 skeptical scientists, the world can finally hear the voices of the "silent majority" of scientists.

(http://ff.org/index.php?option=com_content&task=view&id=406&Itemid

SOCIALISM AND THE WAR AGAINST GOD

When the United States of America was established, it came into being as a theistic nation, a nation founded upon Christian principles. It was not an Muslim nation, nor an atheistic nation, but a Christian nation. Today when fools cry, "separation of church and state" they do so in ignorance and malice. We have separation of church and state in that there is not state church. What these secular humanists want is separation of God and state!

They demand to have the ten commandments removed from court houses and want prayer banned in our schools. And now Christmas and manger scenes are under attack. I know about the origin of Christmas and never thought much of manger scenes. Although there is not the slightest probability that the actual birth date of Christ was December 25th, we must realize that the attack upon Christmas is not an attack upon the Catholic Church, but upon ALL Christianity and our Lord Jesus Christ.

Every Christian in the United States has an enemy in the White House. Not only do we have powerful politicians against us, there are numerous atheist, humanist, and Marxist organizations against us and our God. Organizations like the Americans for Civil Liberties Union and the Southern Poverty Law Center are always on the side of the ungodly. These secular humanist organizations and others like them have put forward that our American republic was founded on Greco-Roman forms instead of Biblical principles. The following quote will dismiss that ill-founded conception.

During the formation of this nation one of our founding fathers deemed to be the least religious of the group made this remarkable plea for prayer:

Thursday, June 28th, 1787. James Madison recorded the proceedings in his Journal of the Federal Convention, Volume I, page 259. Here are Franklin's words, directed to George Washington.

Doctor Franklin: Mr. President, The small progress we have made after four or five weeks close attendance and continual reasonings with each other — our different sentiments on almost every question, several of the last producing as many noes as ayes, is, methinks, a melancholy proof of the imperfection of the human understanding. We indeed seem to feel our own want of political wisdom, since we have been running about in search of it. We have gone back to ancient history for models of government, and examined the different forms of those republics, having been formed with seeds of their own dissolution, now no longer exists. And we have viewed modern states all round Europe, but find none of their constitutions suitable to our circumstances. In this situation of this Assembly, groping as it were in the dark to find political truth, and scarce able to distinguish it when presented to us, how has it happened, Sir, that we have not hitherto once thought of humbly applying to the Father of lights, to illuminate our understandings? In the beginning of the contest with Great Britain, when we were sensible of danger, we had daily prayer in this room for the divine protection. Our prayers, Sir, were heard, and they were graciously answered. All of us who were engaged in the struggle must have observed frequent instances of a superintending Providence in our favor. To that kind Providence we owe this happy opportunity of consulting in peace on the means of establishing our future national felicity. And have we now forgotten that powerful friend? Or do we imagine that we no longer need his

assistance? I have lived, Sir, a long time, and the longer I live, the more convincing proofs I see of this truth, *that God governs in the affairs of men* [emphasis mine] And if a sparrow cannot fall to the ground without his knowledge, is it probable that an empire can rise without his aid? We have been assured, Sir, in the sacred writings, that except the Lord build the House they labour in vain those that build it." I firmly believe this; and I also believe that without his concurring aid we shall succeed in this political building no better than the Builders of Babel: We shall be divided by our little partial local interest; our projects will be confounded; and we ourselves shall become a reproach and by word down to future ages. And what is worse, mankind may hereafter, from this unfortunate instance, despair of establishing governments by human wisdom, and leave it to chance, war and conquest. I therefore beg leave to move that henceforth prayers imploring the assistance of Heaven, and its blessings on our deliberations, be held in this Assembly every morning before we proceed to business, and that one or more of the clergy of this city be requested to officiate in that service. (http://vftonline.org/EndTheWall/Franklin-prayer.htm)
The Debates in the Several Conventions, on the Adoption of the Federal Constitution, Jonathan Elliot, editor (Washington: Printed for the Editor, 1836), Vol. II, p. 2, Massachusetts Convention, January 9, 1788.

Franklin was known as a "deist." Nonetheless, these are not the words of a true deist. Perhaps God had been working upon him through the instrument of the great evangelist, George Whitefield, for whom he had much admiration. When one reflects on the moral fiber make-up of our founding fathers, it seems implausible that the United States of America has Barack Hussein Obama and his socialist czars at the helm. But the contamination goes deeper than Barack Hussein Obama. The following anonymous quote cuts to the heart of the matter:

> The danger to America is not Barack Obama but a citizenry capable of entrusting a man like him with the presidency. It will be easier to limit and undo the follies of an Obama presidency than to restore the necessary common sense and good judgment to a depraved electorate willing to have such a man for their president.
>
> The problem is much deeper and far more serious than Mr. Obama, who is a mere symptom of what ails us. Blaming the prince of the fools should not blind anyone to the vast confederacy of fools that made him their prince.
>
> The republic can survive a Barack Obama, who is after all, merely a fool. It is less likely to survive a multitude of fools such as those who made him their president.

Perhaps we as a nation are seeing the judgment of God. When Israel departed from God and homosexuals came out of their closets judgment fell upon the nation. Isaiah 3:1-4, 9, 12:

> *For, behold, the Lord, the Lord of hosts, doth take away from Jerusalem and from Judah the stay and the staff, the whole stay of bread, and the whole stay of water, the mighty man, and the man of war, the judge, and the prophet, and the prudent, and the ancient, the captain of fifty, and the honourable man, and counsellor, and the cunning artificer, and the eloquent orator.*
>
> *And I will give children to be their princes, and babes shall rule over them. The shew of their countenance*

doth witness against them; and they declare their sin as Sodom, they hide it not. Woe unto their soul! for they have rewarded evil unto themselves. As for my people, children are their oppressors, and women rule over them. O my people, they lead thee cause thee to err, and destroy the way of thy paths."

In Luke 11:23 our Lord declares, **"He that is not with me is against me; and he that gathereth not with me scattereth."** Our Lord categorically denies any possibility of neutrality regarding his person or His work. Every individual must be either for Christ or against Him. A school is either for Christ or against Him. A political party is in support of Him or against Him. This is true of the White House, the Congress, the Supreme Court. Those who are not unequivocally for Christ are in opposition to Him.

Those who are against Christ have Christ against them! What happens to those who fail to show allegiance to our Lord? The answer is in Psalms 2:12: **"Kiss the Son, lest he be angry, and ye perish from the way, when his wrath is kindled but a little. . . ."**

In the 1950s there was a television show that predicted the coming age of the computer. In this program there was a very large computer about the size of a small house. In this story our economy, our currency, and our government had collapsed. Society was in chaos, turmoil, and anarchy. People were behaving like wild beasts and there appeared to be no hope for the future of mankind. No one had an answer that could solve the multitude of tribulations. The brightest minds were bankrupt when a solution was needed. At last, someone came up with the idea of seeking a way out from the computer. All of the facts regarding our predicament were fed into the central processing unit of the computer along with an appeal for a remedy. The computer clicked and clanked and lights flashed on and off as about twenty-five people in the room were waiting in great apprehension to learn if the computer could offer an answer to save civilization. Finally, after hours of waiting, the computer made a different sound and printing was appearing on a large sheet of paper— The answer!

1. Thou shalt have no other gods before me.

2. Thou shalt not make unto thee any graven image.

3. Thou shalt not take the name of the Lord thy God in vain.

4. Remember the Sabbath Day, to keep it holy.

5. Honour thy father and thy mother.

6. Thou shalt do no murder.

7. Thou shalt not commit adultery.

8. Thou shalt not steal.

9. Thou shalt not lie.

10. Thou shalt not covet.

APPENDIX A

Carroll Quigley

Carroll Quigley (1910 –1977) was a historian with knowledge of a wide range of subjects who was particularly interested in studying the progress of civilizations. A native of Boston, Quigley attended Harvard, earning B.A, M.A., and Ph.D. degrees in history. Afterwards, he taught at Princeton and Harvard for short tenures. From 1941 until his retirement in 1976 he was employed by the School of Foreign Service at Georgetown University. His obituary in the *Washington Star* reports that numerous alumni of Georgetown's School of Foreign Service declared that his was "the most influential course in their undergraduate careers". Quigley also did consulting work for the U.S. Department of Defense, the U.S. Navy, the Smithsonian Institution, and the House Select Committee on Astronautics and Space Exploration in the 1950s. He was a book reviewer for the *Washington Star* and was a contributor and editorial board member of the periodical, *Current History*. His work stressed "inclusive diversity" to be of major significance in Western Civilization long before the broad term, "diversity" came into being. From the start Quigley was a stern opponent of the Vietnam War. He saw the activities of the *military-industrial complex* (the relationships between governments, national armed forces, and the industrial sector that supports them) as the future downfall of the country.[54]

Future U.S. President Bill Clinton took Quigley's course during his freshman year in the School of Foreign Service at Georgetown and earned a 'B' as his final grade in the two-semester course. When William Jefferson Clinton kicked off his presidential campaign in a speech at Georgetown in 1991, he proclaimed that Quigley was a vital influence on his aspirations and political

---

[54] "Obituary," *The Washington Star*: section B, page 4, Jan. 6, 1977.

philosophy. Once again, when Clinton made his acceptance speech to the 1992 Democratic National Convention, he mentioned Quigley:[55]

> As a teenager, I heard John Kennedy's summons to citizenship. And then, as a student at Georgetown, I heard that call clarified by a professor named Carroll Quigley, who said to us that America was the greatest Nation in history because our people had always believed in two things–that tomorrow can be better than today and that every one of us has a personal moral responsibility to make it so.[56]

Although writing about secret societies was not the main thrust of Professor Quigley's work, it was his writing on this very topic that made Quigley famous.[9] Quigley asserted that secret societies have played a considerable role in the history of the modern world. This is unique due to the fact that the majority of reputable academic historians have professed skepticism about conspiracy theories.[57]

The Milner Group: Written in 1949, *The Anglo-American Establishment: From Rhodes to Cliveden* was published four years after Quigley's death. In this book, Quigley professed to trace the history of a secret society founded in 1891 by Cecil Rhodes and Alfred Milner. "The Society of the Elect" was composed of an inner circle and an outer circle.[58] The society as a whole did not

---

[55] Scott McLemee (Dec. 1996). "The Quigley Cult," *George Magazine* 1 (10): 94, 96.

[56] Bill Clinton, "Acceptance Speech," Democratic National Convention, New York, NY, July 16, 1992. Full text.

[57] Scott McLemee (Dec. 1996). "The Quigley Cult," *George Magazine* 1 (10): 96, 98.

[58] Seymour Martin Lipset and Earl Raab (1970). *The Politics of Unreason*. Harper & Row.

have a firm name. At different times, this society has been known as Milner's Kindergarten, the Round Table Group, the Rhodes crowd, *The Times* crowd, the All Souls group, and as the Cliveden set.

> "... I have chosen to call it the Milner group. Those persons who have used the other terms, or heard them used, have not generally been aware that all these various terms referred to the same Group. It is not easy for an outsider to write the history of a secret group of this kind, but, since no insider is going to do it, an outsider must attempt it. It should be done, for this Group is, as I shall show, one of the most important historical facts of the twentieth century."[59]

Quigley gives this group credit for quite a few historical events: the Jameson Raid, the Second Boer War, the founding of the Union of South Africa, the changeover from the British Empire to the Commonwealth of Nations, as well as many other twentieth century British foreign policy resolutions.[60]

Tragedy and Hope was the large one-volume "history" of the twentieth century that Quigley published in 1966 in which he traces the development of **Round Table Groups**. Quigley states that he has actually been in direct contact with this organization:

> This radical Right fairy tale, is now an accepted folk myth in many groups in America, pictured the recent history of the United States, in regard to domestic reform and in foreign affairs, as a well-organized plot by extreme Left-wing elements.... This myth, like all fables,

---

Ted Goertzel (1994). "Belief in Conspiracy Theories". *Political Psychology* 15: 733–744. http://www.crab.rutgers.edu/~goertzel/conspire.doc.

[59] Carroll Quigley, *The Anglo-American Establishment: From Rhodes to Cliveden.* p.ix.

[60] Ibid. ix, 3.

> does in fact have a modicum of truth. There does exist, and has existed for a generation, an international Anglophile network operates, to some extent, in the way the Radical right believes the Communists act. **In fact, this network, we may identify as the Round Table Groups, has no aversion to cooperating with the Communists, or any other group, and frequently does so.** I know of the operation of this network because I have studied it for twenty years and was permitted for two years, in the early 1960's, to examine its papers and secret records. I have no aversion to it or to most of its aims and have, for much of my life, been close to it and to many of its instruments. I have objected, both in the past and recently, to a few of its policies... but in general my chief difference of opinion is that it wishes to remain unknown, and I believe its role in history is significant enough to be known.[61]

Quigley gives an epigrammatic account of other secret societies in *Tragedy and Hope*, consisting of a conglomerate of bankers of several countries who form the Bank for International Settlements. Their aim is to "create a world system of financial control in private hands able to dominate the political system of each country and the economy of the world as a whole."[62]

The leaders of this group were, according to Quigley, both Cecil Rhodes and Alfred Milner from 1891-1902. When Rhodes died in 1902, Milner was alone in the role of leadership until his own death in 1925. Lionel Curtis was at the helm from 1925 to 1955; Robert H. (Baron) Brand from 1955 to 1963, and Adam D. Marris from 1963 until the time of the writing of *Tragedy and Hope*. This group also worked through the associated inter-relation of certain

---

[61] Carroll Quigley, *The Anglo-American Establishment: From Rhodes to Cliveden*. New York: Books in Focus. p. 5.
[62] Carroll Quigley, *Tragedy and Hope: A History of the World in Our Time*. New York: Macmillan. pp.949–950.

"front groups," which included the Royal Institute of International Affairs, the Institute of Pacific Relations, and the Council on Foreign Relations. Quigley reported that after 1963 the organization's activities were "greatly reduced."[63]

Did Carroll Quigley realize to what extent his book would grab the interest of conspiracy theorists? The matter is open for deliberation. Not long after its publication, others grabbed hold of Quigley's claims and circulated them to a wider readership.[64]

In 1970 W. Cleon Skousen published *The Naked Capitalist: A Review and Commentary on Dr. Carroll Quigley's Book "Tragedy and Hope"*. The first third of this book is excerpts from *Tragedy and Hope*, intermingled with interpretations by Skousen. Skousen dissects Quigley's accounts of the Milner Group's activities, the Communist Party, the Institute of Pacific Relations, and the Council on Foreign Relations. According to Skousen, each of these is but a facet of one conspiracy.[65]

John Birch Society spokesman Gary Allen, published *None Dare Call It Conspiracy* in 1971. It immediately became a bestseller. Throughout his book, Allen referred to *Tragedy and Hope* as his authority for the existence of an assortment of conspiracies. Allen, like Skousen, believed the conspiracies in Quigley's book were branches of one large conspiracy, and also connected them to the Bilderbergers and tied them to Richard Nixon.[66]

---

[63] Ibid. pp.132, 950–952.
[64] Scott McLemee (Dec. 1996). "The Quigley Cult." *George Magazine* 1 (10): 96, 98.
[65] W. Cleon Skousen (1970). *The Naked Capitalist: A Review and Commentary on Dr. Carroll Quigley's Book "Tragedy and Hope."* 1–6, 38–44 (communists), 6–24 (bankers), 26–38 (Rhodes and Milner), 45–48 (IPR), 50–57 (CFR).
[66] Gary Allen with Larry Abraham *None Dare Call It Conspiracy*. 12-13, 39, 42, 52, 57, 59, 79-82, 85.

Numerous writers who aver the existence of potent conspiracies list Quigley as their source of authority. Jim Marrs cites Quigley in his book *Rule By Secrecy*, in which he describes a conspiracy connecting the Milner Group, Skull and Bones, the Trilateral Commission, the Bavarian Illuminati, and the Knights Templar. Marrs' work was used as by Oliver Stone in his film *JFK*.[67]

Pat Robertson in his book, *The New World Order* also cites Quigley as the last word on a great conspiracy. Conservative activist Phyllis Schlafly has claimed that Bill Clinton owed his success in the political realm to the quest of the "world government" outline he learned from Quigley.[68]

In his book *The Creature from Jekyll Island: A Second Look at the Federal Reserve*, G. Edward Griffin depended on Quigley for knowledge about the Federal Reserve and the interconnection of a secret society called the Milner group.[69]

---

[67] Jim Marrs, *Rule By Secrecy: The Hidden History that Connects the Trilateral Commission, the Freemasons, and the Great Pyramids*. 7, 84, 86-89, 109.

[68] Scott McLemee (Dec. 1996). "The Quigley Cult". *George Magazine* 1 (10): 98.

[69] G. Edward Griffin, *The Creature from Jekyll Island: A Second Look at the Federal Reserve*. California: American Media.

APPENDIX B

I embarked upon writing a book on socialism only somewhat convinced of the *conspiracy theory* to explain events on the political and economic scene of the world. Well aware that conspiracy theories are viewed with skepticism by mainstream academics and often ridiculed as being fanatical, I yet became fully persuaded of not-so-secret societies or orders that rule the governments of the human race. They are not always one-hundred percent successful, but they unquestionably have moved us closer to a global government. There is little doubt in my mind that they manipulate the White House and our Congress.

I do believe that there are assemblages such as the International Bankers, the Council on Foreign Relations (CFR), the Trilateral Commission, the Illuminati, the Milner Group, and like factions attempt to have influence over nations.

It is my conviction that behind the regimes of this world is a truly invisible manipulation of wicked spirits under command of Satan. Our only comfort is to know that God has Satan on a chain and he is limited as to his power and activity.

My many years of study of the Bible and Christian Theology persuades me that a branch of Theology known as Angelology must be taught in layman's terms.

It would not be very enlightening to have an understanding of the secret agencies attempt to control governments without knowing about the Invisible Government. If the Lord is willing, a small book on this subject will be forthcoming.

APPENDIX C

THE PULPIT: THE MORAL CONSCIENCE OF THE NATION?

Dr. W. R. Downing

Silicon Valley, California

Is the pulpit the moral conscience of the nation? There are Christians, pastors, theologians and religious writers in our day who blame the American pulpit for our present moral crisis. We are told that if ministers had preached the true gospel, declared God's Word and the Moral Law against the increasing evil of the times, we might not be in the sad state we witness today. Can such a charge be true? We are of this opinion.

There are several considerations: first, there is national judgment for national sin, and often the righteous must suffer with the wicked (Gen. 15:16; Lev. 18:24–28; Dt. 7:1; 18:12; Lam. 1:1–5:22). The nation of Israel serves as an example of a given nation was judged for its sins. God devastated his own covenant people by bringing upon them various enemies (Judg. 2:11–16; 3:12–14; 4:1–3; 6:1ff; 13:1), and finally, the Assyrians and Chaldeans, nations more wicked and fierce than themselves (Isa. 10:5–15; Lam. 1–3; Hab. 1). Although no other nation was in such a covenant relationship with God as was Israel, yet this moral principle remains applicable to every nation (Psa. 9:17 The text designates all nations, making this a universal principle in the Divinely–ordained moral order.)

History witnesses to the fact that a nation degenerates first spiritually, then morally, and then socially and finally, politically. Morality by necessity must have a spiritual foundation; otherwise it is based on either tradition or the relativism of mere human consensus. Society, once morally blind and utterly relativistic, will morally and politically bow to the tyranny of the majority. There needs to be a national moral conscience, and this by necessity must be spiritual. What other source than men of God who care called to faithfully proclaim the truth?

Divine judgment has never been averted simply because a nation has considered itself to be in a special relationship with God. The modern American idea of "God and Country" is presently without sufficient foundation. So is the idea that God will bless America regardless of her national sins. We are officially a secularized society. God and morality have only a token place. A government refuses to capitally punish murderers (Numbers 35:32–33) or sanctions and even sponsors abortion and homosexuality cannot in any sense be considered immune to Divine judgment. As to the former, man was created in the image of God, and this image is inseparable from the most elemental human life (Psa. 139:13–16). Abortion is murder. As to the latter, homosexuality is a perversion of the God–ordained order and brings down Divine wrath (Lev. 18:22; 20:13; Rom. 1:21–32). To think that God will bless America despite her national sins is to think that God is devoid of moral character and his Word is irrelevant; it is to believe in the "god" of one's imagination (Rom. 1:18–25). It is the pulpit's responsibility to proclaim the one true God and his moral character.

Second, is it legitimate to apply the situation of Israel (2 Chron. 7:14) and the Old Testament prophets, who were to decry Israel's national sins (Isaiah 58:1), to our national history and present situation? For the rationale of preaching against national sins, refer to chapter three of "The Preacher as a Patriot," from the book *The*

Preacher and His Models by James Stalker of Vestavia Hills, Alabama, Solid Ground Christian Books, 2003.

On the one hand, we are not a covenant people as was Israel, yet on the other, this nation is unique in history, as it was largely founded on Christian principles we have utterly abandoned as a secularized society. Although not all of our Founding Fathers were Christians, yet every one of them, Christian or Deist, presupposed the moral character of God, and most assumed the veracity of the Bible and the authority of the Moral Law as expressed in the Ten Commandments. Our Founding Fathers knew that this form of government—a constitutional republic—would not be practicable apart from the truth and morality of Christianity. Surely, such a nation must be judged severely, according to the light it has received!

Third, our Lord describes Christians in general as "the light of the world" and "the salt of the earth" (Matt. 5:13–14). Matt. 5:13–14. References to believers as "light" and "salt" implies that Christianity is to be a preserving, illuminating, and exposing element within society. They are to make a discernable moral difference.

This certainly implies that as Christians, we are to have a determining effect upon the society in which we live. Further, the behavior of believers toward one another and toward men in general is to have a profound effect upon this world (Matt. 5:14–16; Jn. 13:34–35; Phil. 2:14–15; 1 Pet. 2:11–15). A godly remnant may serve to keep back national judgment upon a given people. Had there been ten righteous men in Sodom, the judgment of God would have been averted (Gen. 18:20–32).

Fourth, the history of the American pulpit has been varied. There have always been men of God who would not compromise the truth of the Bible. The Gospel has been faithfully preached and the Law of God declared so that a biblical morality has been impressed upon many congregations. God has blessed this country with times of revival and spiritual awakening repeatedly, even in the worst of political and economic times. One has only to consider the first and second "Great Awakenings" (1734–50, 1793–1840) that changed the moral climate of this country and the British Isles, as well as the "Great Prayer Revival" of 1857–58 which came during the great financial crash of 1857. A great revival occurred during the War Between the States in 1861–65, and the Welsh Revival of 1904 changed the moral climate of Wales (Tracy, Joseph, *The Great Awakening.* 433).

But there has also been a slow process of Spiritual degeneration and consequent secularization. The frontier Methodist revivals of the early 1800s gave us "perfectionist" teachings and modified the reality of the Christian experience. The "New Measures" of Charles G. Finney began the slide into the "easy–believeism" and "decisionism" of our day with its psychological conversions and unscriptural methodology. Liberalism has enabled unconverted men to occupy influential pulpits. Dispensationalism has added its inherent antinomianism to this admixture, and silenced the preaching of the Moral Law in evangelical thinking. It has also brought into some Christian circles the idea that one should not become involved in the political or even the social process because of the imminent return of the Lord. In this generation, evangelical Christianity has largely become a "pop culture" far removed from godly worship and the faithful preaching of the Word of God. Sin is now almost irrelevant, holiness is optional, worship has largely become entertainment, social programs have become divorced from a gospel motivation, psychology has replaced theology and worship teams have replaced the Gospel preacher.

The fault of such degeneration and departure from the Word of God must be laid at the feet of those whose call it is to faithfully proclaim the Word of God. As goes the pulpit, so goes the pew. The New Testament Gospel Preacher is the successor to the Old Testament prophet. He is to faithfully declare the Word of God to the people in the power of the Holy Spirit (Isa. 58:1; Hos. 6:5; Jn. 16:8–11). The preachers of the New Testament spoke out about public crime (Acts 2:22–23; 3:14–15), the open immorality of national leaders (Mk. 6:16–20) and were not slack to point to the prevalent sins of governors (Acts 24:24–25). That the fault lies with the pulpit may be seen in the following principle: "The prophets prophesy falsely, and the priests bear rule by their means; and my people love to have it so: and what will ye do in the end thereof?" (Jer. 5:31).

We stand more in need of revival and spiritual awakening in this day than at any previous time of our national history. The truth of God must be declared from the pulpit; it is our great responsibility—and from the pulpit to the people of God, and from the people of God to society.

Bibliography

Allen Gary with Larry Abraham. *None Dare Call It Conspiracy.* Rossmoor, CA: Concord Press, 1971.

Bailey, Thomas A. *The American Pageant: A History of the Republic, 3rd Edition,* Boston, D. C. Health and Sons, 1967.

Bullitt, William C. and "Sigmund Freud." *Thomas Woodrow Wilson: A Psychological Study* London: Weidenfeld & Nicolson, (1966).

Brown, James E and Wolf, Harold A. *Economics, Principles and Practices,* Columbus. Ohio: Charles E. Merrill Publishing Company.

Beversluis, N. H. *Christian Philosophy of Education,* Grand Rapids, MI,: National Union of Christian Schools, 1971.

Berryhill, Dale A. *The Liberal Contradiction: How Contemporary Liberalism Violates Its Own Principles and Endangers Its Own Goals,* Lafayette, Louisiana: Huntington House Publishers, 1994.

Curran, Francis X. *The Churches and the Schools.* Chicago, Illinois, Loyola University Press, 1954.

Dabney, R. L. *Women's Rights,* Spout Spring, VA: Society for Southern and Biblical Studies, 2004.

DiLorenzo, Thomas J. *Hamilton's Curse,* New York: Crown Forum, 2008.

DiLorenzo, Thomas J. *How Capitalism Saved America,* New York: Three Rivers Press, 2004.

Fellman, Michael. *Citizen Sherman: A Life of William Tecumseh Sherman.* Lawrence Kansas: University of Kansas Press, 1995.

Fleming, Thomas. *Socialism,* Tarrytown, NJ: Marshall Cavendish Benchmark, 2008.

Folsom, Burton W. Jr. *The Myth of the Robber Barons,* Herndon, VA: Young America's Foundation, 1987, 1991, 1996, 2003, 2007.

French, William M. *America's Educational Tradition.* Boston, D. C. Heath and Company, 1964.

Griffin Des. *Midnight Messenger of Cultural Marxism*, Colton, Colorado: Emissary Publications.

Griffin G. Edward . *The Creature from Jekyll Island: A Second Look at the Federal Reserve*. California: American Media, 1994.

Gross, Martin L. *A Call for Revolution,* New York: Random House, 1993.

Gross, Martin L. *The Political Racket.* New York: Random House.1996.

Gross, Martin L., *Washington Waste from A to Z,* New York, Bantam Books, 1992.

Grose, Peter. *Continuing the Inquiry,* New York: Council on Foreign Relations, 1996, 2006.

Hodge, A. A. *Popular Lectures on Theological Themes.* Philadelphia: Presbyterian Board of Publications, 1889.

Hodge, Charles. *Systematic Theology*, Vol.   III, Grand Rapids: William B. Eerdmans Publishing,

Ingram, T. Robert, *The World Under God's Law,* Houston, Texas: St. Thomas Press, 1970.

Keynes, John Maynard. Elizabeth Johnson and Donald Moggridge, eds. *The Collected Writings of John Maynard Keynes*. Cambridge: Cambridge University Press, 1982.

Kennedy, Walter and Al Benson, Jr., *Red Republicans and Lincoln's Marxists,* Lincoln, Nebraska: iUniverse Publishing Company, 2007.

Kershner, Howard E. *Dividing the Wealth,* Old Greenwich Connecticut: Devin-Adair Company, 1957.

Lee, Francis Nigel. *A Christian Introduction to the History of Philosophy,* Nutley, New Jersey: Craig Press, 1969.

Lipset, Seymour Martin and Earl Raab. *The Politics of Unreason*. New York: Harper & Row, 1970.

Marrs, Jim . *Rule By Secrecy: The Hidden History that Connects the Trilateral Commission, the Freemasons, and the Great Pyramids*. New York: Harper Collins, 2000.

Martin, Rose L. *Fabian Freeway: High Road to Socialism in the U.S.A.,* Washington, D. C. : The Heritage Foundation, 1966.

Morgan, G. Campbell, *The Ten Commandments,* London and Edinburgh, Fleming H. Revell Company, 1901.

North, Gary. *An Introduction to Christian Economics*, Nutley, NJ: The Craig Press, 1973.

Owen, John. *The Death of Death in the Death of Christ*, London: Banner of Truth Trust, 1963.

Pink, Arthur W. *The Ten Commandments,* Swengel PA, Reiner Publications, 1971,

Quigley, Carroll. *The Anglo-American Establishment: From Rhodes to Cliveden.* New York: Books in Focus, 1981.

Quigley, Carroll *Tragedy and Hope: A History of the World in Our Time.* New York: Macmillan, 1966.

Reeves, Thomas C. *The Life and Times of Joe McCarthy.* 1982.

Rogers, Adrian. *Ten Secrets for a Successful Family,* Wheaton, Illinois: Crossway Books and Bibles, 1998.

Roper, Gary Lee. *Antebellum Slavery: An Orthodox Christian View,* Philadelphia, Xlibris Publishing Company, 2009.

Rushdooney, Rousas J. *By What Standard*, Philadelphia: Presbyterian and Reformed Publishing Company, 1971.

Rushdooney, Rousas J. *The Biblical Philosophy of History,* Nutley, N. J.: Presbyterian and Reformed Publishing Company, 1969.

Rushdooney R. J. *Law and Liberty*, Nutley, N. J.: The Craig Press, 1971.

Rushdooney R. J. *The Foundations of Social Order,* Presbyterian and Reformed Publishing Company, 1968.

This Independent Republic. Nutley, N. J.: The Craig Press, 1964.

Rushdooney, R. J. *Intellectual Schizophrenia,* Presbyterian and Reformed Publishing Company, 1971.

Rushdooney R. J. *Law and Liberty*, Nutley, N. J.: The Craig Press, 1971.

Rushdooney R. J. *The Nature of the American System*, Nutley, N. J.: The Craig Press, 1965.

Rushdooney R. J. *The Messianic Character of American Education,* Nutley, New Jersey: The Craig Press, 1968.

Rushdooney, R. J. *Politics of Guilt and Pity,* Nutley, N. J.: Craig Press, 1970.

Singer, Gregg C. *A Theological Interpretation of American History,* Nutley, NJ: Craig Press,1969.

Skousen, W. Cleon. *The Naked Capitalist.* Salt Lake City: The Reviewer. 1970.

Stang, Alan. *It's Very Simple.* Belmont, MA, Western Islands, 1965.

Stang, Alan. *The Actor: The True Story of John Foster Dulles, Secretary of State, 1953-1959,* Boston & Los Angeles: Western Islands, 1968.

Steele, David and Thomas, Curtis. *The Five Points of Calvinism,* Philadelphia: Presbyterian and Reformed Publishing Company, 1967.

Towns, Elmer. *The Christian Hall of Fame,* Grand Rapids: Baker Book House, 1971.

Wallbank, Walter T., et. al. *Civilization, vol. 2,* Scott, Foresman and Co, 1942.

Warmke, Roman F., *Consumer Economic Problems, Cincinnati,* Ohio, South-Western Publishing Co. , 1971.

Wickliffe, Vennard B. Sr., *The Federal Reserve Hoax Exposed,* 1973.

Watson, Thomas. *The Ten Commandments.* London: Banner of Truth Trust, 1890,1958, 1965.

Wilson, Stephen D. *The Bankruptcy of America,* Germantown, TN: Ridge Mills Press, 1992.

Woods, Thomas E. Jr., *Meltdown,* Washington, D. C., Regnery Press, 2009.

INDEX

Abraham Lincoln, 11, 20, 21, 23, 26, 69, 77
Adam Smith, 41, 45
Alfred Milner, 198
Alger Hiss, 136
Allan Pinkerton, 20
Andrew Jackson, 27, 42

Benjamin Franklin, 12, 79, 117
Black Liberation Theology, 54

Carl Schurz, 20
CARROLL QUIGLEY, 3, 36, 38, 199, 200
Chaiang Kai-Shek 37
Charles A. Dana, 20
Charles Darwin, 96
Charles G. Finney, 120
Che Guevara, 57
Christian Socialism 7
Communism (defined) 7
Council on Foreign Relations, 29, 30, 36, 38, 124, 153, 201, 202, 204, 209

direct taxes, 79
Dean Acheson, 37
Douglas MacArthur, 37, 38

Edward Bellamy, 24, 25
Edward M. House, 28, 29
Eminent Domain, 73

Fabians, 26

Fabian Society, 7
Fabianism, 47, 129
Feminism, 19
"Forty-Eighters," 20
Francis Bellamy, 24, 25
Franklin D. Roosevelt, 29-36, 51, 67
free trade, 44, 45
Friedrich von Hayek, 44

Henry George, 25, 26
Herbert Hoover, 30
hidden taxes, 79, 80
Horace Mann, 12, 88, 90, 91, 92, 93, 103, 120
Humanist Manifesto, 94, 95, 97, 98

indirect taxes, 79
It Takes a Village, 110

Jacobins, 12
James H. Thornwell, 12
Jane Addams, 132
James Madison, 42, 190,
James H. Thornwell, 12, 19
Jeremy Bentham, 110
John Adams, 160
John Dewey, 25, 93, 94, 99
John Foster Dulles, 29, 135, 136, 138, 212
John Maynard Keynes, 33, 46, 47, 48, 49, 50, 51
John Ruskin, 110

Karl Marx, 7, 8, 20, 21, 23, 95
League of Nations, 30
Kenneth Goff 154, 155
Keynes, see John Maynard Keynes
Leon Trotsky, 24, 28
Ludwig von Mises, 44
Margaret Thatcher, 49, 163
Martin Luther King, Jr. 24, 39, 40
Milton Friedman, 44, 105

National Council of Churches, 120, 123, 124, 125, 126, 129, 136, 138, 139, 141, 142, 144, 146, 148
No Child Left Behind, 64, 103, 104, 105, 106, 107
Norman Thomas, 131, 132
New Deal, 33, 41, 78
Norman Thomas, 4, 24, 131, 132
Nelson Aldrich, 29

original intent law, 95

Plato, 6, 95
Philip Dru, 29

Quigley, see Carroll Quigley

relative law, 95
relativism, 95, 96, 206
reparations, 68, 69, 70, 146, 147

(Plato's), 6, 84, 88, 110
Richard Cobden, 45
Rick Warren, 154, 155, 156
Robert Lewis Dabney, 113, 114, 119
Robert Owen, 6, 10, 88, 92,
Robert E. Lee, 87

Samuel T. Francis, 5

Theodore Parker, 9, 119
theory of evolution, 99
(The) Nation Magazine, 24
Thomas Jefferson, 4, 27, 73, 87, 88, 158
Thomas Paine, 115, 116
Tragedy and Hope, 36, 38, 201, 202,
Transcendental, 119

Unitarian, 12, 88, 119, 141

Wealth of Nations, 45

Werner von Braun, 101
William Tecumseh Sherman, 9, 10
William Lloyd Garrison, 131

Woodrow Wilson, 28, 29, 30, 39, 76